How to Get a
You Love

How to Get a Job You Love

2021–22 Edition

John Lees

 Open University Press

Open University Press
McGraw-Hill Education
8th Floor, 338 Euston Road
London
England
NW1 3BH

email: enquiries@openup.co.uk
world wide web: www.openup.co.uk

and Two Penn Plaza, New York, NY 10121-2289, USA

A catalogue record of this book is available from the British Library

ISBN-13: 9781526847980
ISBN-10: 1526847980
eISBN: 9781526847997

Library of Congress Cataloging-in-Publication Data
CIP data applied for

Typeset by Transforma Pvt. Ltd., Chennai, India

Printed in Great Britain by Bell and Bain Ltd, Glasgow

PRAISE FOR *HOW TO GET A JOB YOU LOVE*

"This is so much more than a 'how to' book – it also brings the reader expertly and seamlessly through the much bigger career questions of career identity and purpose, and how to fully appreciate and utilise the best of your skills and talents, so that you not only progress in your career search, but also learn to thrive each step of the way. John's in-depth knowledge of the marketplace, global and local trends, and his unrivalled position as a Careers expert means that he speaks with authenticity and authority on the tricky prospect that is reinventing yourself and reinvigorating your career. Read it, act on the advice, and you will see your career flourish."
Sophie Rowan, Chartered Work and Organisational Psychologist, Executive Coach, and bestselling author of *Brilliant Career Coach*

"This is THE definitive careers book which just keeps on getting better. I recommend it to listeners on my podcast and to my coaching clients, as it is up to date and provides clear, accessible and engaging career guidance which will help readers no matter what stage they are in their job seeking journey. Life is too short to spend your time doing a job you don't enjoy. This book gives you the practical step-by-step skills, exercises and strategies you will need to get the job you'll love."
James Curran, Graduate career coach and podcast host at www.graduatejobpodcast.com

"I love this book and have both used it as a useful guide and recommended it to clients since it was first published. It's full of practical guidance, insightful ideas and creative tools to help break through the impasse that often accompanies career decision making. When it first emerged, it stood out for its straightforward and accessible content grounded in the reality of the world of work. Today the clarity of this book is more important than ever."

**Marie McManamon, Career Consultant,
Clearcut Careers, Dublin**

"I frequently recommend job seekers or those at a career crossroads to read *How to Get a Job You Love* as it offers practical and easily accessible advice from someone with vast experience in the area."

**Joëlle Warren MBE, DL, Executive Chair,
Warren Partners**

"I love this book, deservedly a classic in the world of career transition. I wholeheartedly recommend it to anyone finding themselves at a crossroads in their work life. This new edition is bang up to date and is needed now more than ever at a time of huge change and uncertainty - when people are asking big questions about the future of work and how to navigate it. This edition is packed with valuable information. John Lees is a guru of the career change world. His experience and wisdom radiate from every page."

**Marianne Craig, ICF Master Coach,
Co-Founder Firework Career Coaching Company**

"John Lees will appeal to people internationally, from the East and the West. For more than 15 years, I have been using the ideas, strategies, tools and resources outlined in this book (and previous editions) with students, graduates and professionals enabling them to navigate their career transitions with greater confidence."

**Ajaz Hussain, Career Counsellor,
Global Energy Company, Middle East & 2020
University College London Alumni of the Year**

"John Lees advice on careers is always useful and interesting and often surprising and even fascinating. From getting ahead to changing your career completely, this book is great guide to navigating the treacherous waters of the modern workplace."

Rhymer Rigby, FT journalist and author of *28 Business Thinkers Who Changed The World*

"This is a timely update of an excellent book. John Lees is not just a master of his material, he is a master communicator. Those thinking hard about switching careers in the time of increased 'job fragility' and Coronavirus should start from the superb advice, information and great practical exercises that John provides."
Stuart Robertson, Chartered Psychologist and co-author of the Quintax Personality Questionnaire

"There are dozens of books that will guide you on how to find a job - some useful, some not so much. This book provides up-to-date, grounded, real-world advice and practical tools on how to find a job against a backdrop where technology and hiring processes have changed so much in recent years, and at a time when many people will need support due to the downturn in the market. This book is a great investment in your job-search strategy."
Paul Drew, Career Strategist and Executive Career Lead, London Business School.

"Getting a job that you love may seem impossible especially on a Monday morning! However it is a goal worth putting some thought and effort toward. The world of work is constantly changing so we need to adapt our approach to career management and our mental health and well-being is very much linked to our work environment too. John's book is packed with practical and very balanced advice, tools and insights into how you can get the career you want and want the career you get. This revised edition is even more relevant and useful in a changing employment market and uncertain economic environment."
Gordon McFarland, Global HR Director BCG

"Watch out – this book could turn your life upside down."
Liz Hall, Editor, *Coaching At Work*

"The popularity of John Lees' writing lies in his ability to connect with the sense many people have that they can be more than they currently are and deserve greater job satisfaction than they currently have. What makes his work distinctive is his use of his wide experience in careers coaching to provide tools and ways of thinking that any motivated individual can easily use to take control of their working life."
Carole Pemberton, Career and Executive Coach and author of *Coaching to Solutions*

"An absolute cracker of a book that will quite literally change your life as well as your career. During the coming years, I am certain that we will all be navigating new waters and making choices that might seem inconceivable right now. Whether you face a new job, unexpected change or a complete professional rethink, simply buy this book – and have John by your side sharing his wisdom and expertise as you steer your way back to hope and career confidence."

Kathryn Jackson, New Zealand Leadership Coach and author of *Resilience at Work* and the *Kite Support* wellbeing app

"When I read John's writing, two things happen. First, I feel as if he's standing right there, personally advising me. And second, I always come away thinking over the issue in a new way. It's a rare and very useful, gift."

Sarah Green, Executive Editor, Harvard Business Review

"A positive, practical and readable guide, packed with creative tools and common sense advice from an author who understands careers from all angles. This book will support and encourage you throughout your working life, from making your initial career decision to helping with long term career management. It will challenge your preconceptions of yourself and of the world of work, and help you to a more fulfilling career."

Julia Yates, Programme Director, MSc Organisational Psychology, City, University of London

"John is a regular speaker at AMBA events. His highly practical approach and engaging style of career coaching made him the obvious choice for AMBA's webinar series. Alongside the various editions of *How To Get A Job You Love* and his other titles, business schools repeatedly welcome John to dispense real-world advice to MBA students and alumni. In my own coaching practice John's techniques are enthusiastically actioned by clients as they design (and achieve) their next role either as an in-house promotion or elsewhere. Importantly in these challenging times of Covid-19 this latest edition offers intensely practical advice for the career changes and opportunities that will arise."

Steve Gorton, Enabling Development; Trustee Director - Association of MBAs (2008 – 2015)

This book, like all previous editions,
is dedicated to someone
who has been special to me
for a very long time.

To my wife, Jan,
for giving me space to find out.

Contents

List of exercises

Foreword – in memory of Richard Nelson Bolles

(Dick Bolles wrote this foreword for an earlier edition of the book, before his sad death in March 2017. This text is reprinted with the permission of Dick's estate.)

You would not believe how many career and job-hunting books cross my path each year. New ones appear at my door week by week. All of them have some good ideas, of course, but only a few really stand out. John Lees' classic work is one of those. I cannot recommend it highly enough. It is thorough, inventive, truth-telling and helpful. I have known John, and this book, for a long, long time. John was a student of mine, twice in fact, back when dinosaurs were still roaming the earth. He was already well known for his distinguished career, but since then he has, as we say, gone from strength to strength. We have stayed in touch all these years, in spite of the fact that I live across the pond (in the San Francisco Bay area, to be exact).

He is one of those people in life who is thoroughly worth staying in touch with. His integrity is rock-solid, he is always anxious to help as many people as possible, he is thoroughly grounded in a faith that means something, and he is an expert in his field. You want a book from such a man, you *hope for* a book from such a man. And, thank the good Lord, here it is.

Now used by countless numbers of people, who found themselves helped by the wisdom in these pages, this book is a treasure. Read it, devour it, use it, and find that job you once dreamed about but had almost given up on. Time to revive your dreams. This book will give you chariots to ride.

Richard Nelson Bolles (1927–2017)
Author of *What Color Is Your Parachute?*
A Practical Manual for Job-Hunters and
Career-Changers

About the author

John Lees is one of the UK's best-known career strategists and the author of 15 books on careers and work. *How to Get a Job You Love* regularly tops the list as the bestselling career change handbook by a British author and was twice selected as the WH Smith Business Book of the Month. John's books have been translated into Arabic, Georgian, Polish, Japanese, and Spanish.

John has written careers columns for *Metro* and *People Management*. In 2012, he wrote the introduction to the *Harvard Business Review Guide to Getting the Right Job*. He appears frequently in the national press and his work has been profiled in *Management Today*, *Psychologies*, *Coaching at Work* and *The Sunday Times*. TV appearances include *Back to Work* (BBC Interactive), *Working Lunch* (BBC2), *Dispatches* (Channel 4), *Talking Business (BBC World)*, and *Tonight – How To Get A Job* (ITV). He regularly runs masterclasses for other career coaches, and has delivered career workshops in Australia, Germany, Ireland, New Zealand, Mauritius, Spain, South Africa, Switzerland, and several parts of the USA.

John is a graduate of the universities of Cambridge, London and Liverpool, and has spent his career focusing on the world of work, spending 25 years training recruitment specialists. He is the former Chief Executive of the Institute of Employment Consultants (now the REC) and is an Honorary Fellow of the REC. He served as Joint Chair of the Association of Career Professionals-UK (2011 13), was a founding Board Director of the Career Development Institute, and in March 2016 was elected a NICEC Fellow.

He has consulted for a wide range of organisations including: Boston Consulting Group, The British Council, Careershifters, CIPD, Endsleigh, Gumtree, Harrods, Hiscox, The House of Commons, ICAEW, Imperial College, The Association of MBAs, Lloyds Banking Group, Marks & Spencer, the National Audit Office, Standard Life, Totaljobs, plus business schools across the UK.

Alongside his day job, John serves as an Anglican priest in the Diocese of Exeter. He is a Prebendary of Exeter Cathedral and Bishop's Officer for Self-Supporting Ministry. He is married to the poet and children's writer Jan Dean.

John Lees Associates (www.johnleescareers.com) specialises in helping people to make difficult career decisions – difficult either because they don't know what to do next or because there are barriers in the way.

Career coach training from John Lees

John is part of the team at Firework Coaching, which provides high-impact, ICF-accredited career coach training. Their training is designed to give existing coaches the confidence and credibility to work successfully with people going through career change. It does this through providing a proven framework and set of tools, including many from this book, together with a supportive community of licensed coaches around the world.

Find out more at www.fireworkcoaching.com

Acknowledgements

With age comes, perhaps later than it should, a realisation of those many people I haven't thanked enough.

My gratitude goes to several special people. To Becky Charman for efficiently managing my PR for many years, and to my agent James Wills at Watson, Little for his unstinting support through many projects. I thank Kate Howlett, Managing Consultant at John Lees Associates, for her unfailing encouragement and my brother Andrew Lees for his insights into thinking styles.

I'm aware how many people have worked on this book for the last 20-plus years. My thanks go to my McGraw-Hill editors Clara Heathcock and Eleanor Christie, and to Hannah Kenner for setting the project up. I also want to thank my very first editor, Elizabeth Choules, for getting excited enough to commission it, and to Jane Bartlett and Stuart Mitchell for writing a technical review of the first edition and finding things to like.

I'm grateful to colleagues who have let me road-test ideas with different audiences: Richard Alderson (Careershifters), Mel Barclay and Adi Mechen (LHH Penna), Samantha Brown (ICAEW), Fabian Caton (Totaljobs), Janice Chalmers (Surrey University Business School), Lindsay Comalie and Nicola Pogson (Imperial College), James Curran (Graduate Job Podcast), Paul Drew (London Business School), Liz Dimmock

(Women Ahead), Sarah Jackson (Warwick Business School), Lisa Jones (Officers' Association), Gordon McFarland (BCG), Rob Nathan (CCS), Steve Mirfin (National Audit Office), Wendy Pearson (Durham University Business School), Jessica Taylor-Delaney (Page Group), Nicky Trainor (Organisation Development Institute, NZ), Helen Walker (Bentley), Laura Woodward (Royal Society of Chemistry), and Marie Zimenoff (Career Thought Leaders).

My appreciation goes out to all those who have inspired, encouraged, provided feedback on draft material or asked great questions: Richard Alderson, Gill Best, Jo Bond, Marie Brett, Jim Bright, Julian Childs, Steve Crabb, Jim Currie, Hilary Dawson, Sara Dewar, Zena Everett, Matthias Feist, David Fouracre, Trevor Gilbert, Helen Green, Tudor Humphreys, Ajaz Hussain, Kathryn Jackson, Esi Kpeglo, Stuart Lindenfield, Adi Mechen, Brian McIvor, Rosemary McLean, Derek Osborn, Amiel Osmaston, James Parsons, Bernard Pearce, Carole Pemberton, Daniel Porot, Rhymer Rigby, Stuart Robertson, Valerie Rowles, Philip Sourbut, Natasha Stanley, Hugh Valentine, Joëlle Warren, Ruth Winden and Julia Yates. I would particularly like to thank Gill Frigerio, Anne Futcher, David Herbert, and Magdalen Smith for helping to refine this edition's thinking on vocation. My appreciation to Nicola McGinty (3D Coaching) for teaching me to think of clients as 'thinkers' rather than 'coachees'. I thank the community of NICEC fellows for their collective wisdom.

I'm enormously grateful to my expert guest contributors and to former clients who kindly agreed to be case studies: Will Beale, Melissa Carr, Beth Grant, Simon Ryan, James Voûte, and Mary Wilson.

I take this moment to remember with gratitude two colleagues who are no longer with us. I'm thinking of my friend and publicist Sue Blake who made the first 10 years of being published so much fun, and of course the inspirational teacher Richard Nelson Bolles, author of the world-famous *What Color Is Your Parachute?* My work continues to be inspired by the creativity, wisdom and generosity of Dick's teaching including two summer workshops in Bend, Oregon. He leaves a huge gap in the careers world.

Other careers books by John Lees published by McGraw-Hill Professional

Knockout CV (2013), £11.99, ISBN 978-0077152857
Building on an extensive review of what employers love and hate about CVs, this book provides a wealth of practical tips on CV design and impact, helping you decide which CV format works best for you, and showing you how to write CVs and cover letters that convey your strengths quickly and get you into the interview room.

Knockout Interview (2017), £11.99, ISBN 978-0077189563
The definitive overview of the job interview process and how to prepare for it. Includes a wide range of example questions you will face, and strategies for how to answer them, plus quick-fix solutions if you have an interview tomorrow.

Career Reboot: 24 Tips for Tough Times (2009), £8.99, ISBN 978-0077127589
Packed with quick-read, practical tips for rejuvenating your job search, this book is a must for anyone striking out into a difficult job market after redundancy or simply looking for new opportunities in a difficult market.

Get Ahead in Your New Job (2019), £12.99, ISBN 978-1526847492
A practical guide to help you establish yourself quickly and effectively in a new role, whatever your level in an organisation. In the first 100 days of a new job you have a unique opportunity to shape your work reputation. This book shows you how to hit the ground running and avoid classic mistakes.

How to use this book

Who is this book for?

This book is written for anyone who is trying to make informed decisions about career choice. This book can help if you are:

- wondering how to think about work and careers after the strange world of COVID-19 restrictions
- facing redundancy, and asking 'what do I do next?'
- feeling 'stuck' and looking for new challenges, and wondering 'what on earth can I do?'
- leaving full-time education or returning to work after a break
- deciding how to reinvent yourself mid-career, or in pre-retirement mode
- unemployed and looking for better ways of identifying opportunities
- seeking work and hitting a brick wall with applications
- discouraged because you believe you have little to offer the labour market
- playing with the idea of changing career completely.

How this book might help you

There are many 'how to' books about career change and job search. If you're looking for boxes to tick, 'to do' checklists, model CVs or letters, look at one of the hundreds of books available that will give you an organised, left-brain solution to career management. We all need good advice when it comes to managing our job search. These books work well if you have a clear sense of direction, and all you need is a more effective job search technique. However, they are less effective at answering a familiar request for help: 'I know I want to do something different, but I don't know what it is.' And just as important, the question: 'How do I take the first step towards something new?'

The chapters ahead take a different approach. These pages will encourage you to look differently – at yourself, at the job market, and the way you approach it. This book's aim is to encourage you to think and act differently, so you open doors you wouldn't have expected to open. It will challenge the limitations you put in your own way, and help you discover your strengths. You'll look at the way businesses and individuals reinvent themselves every day, and apply some of that creative thinking and purposeful energy to your career. It will show you how to imagine and discover possibilities. It will show you new ways of exploring. It will encourage you to propel yourself towards a job that feels worth getting up for on a cold Monday morning.

Read on and you will find tools for incremental change, and also strategies for making a bigger transformation. This book aims to unlock your hidden potential and make your waking hours more creative, more meaningful, more enjoyable. Its focus is not on job change for its own sake, but to help you understand yourself better, communicate more effectively, and to take control so that *work works for you.*

This book focuses on the big career question – *what next?* However, you may discover that you don't need to jump ship in order to improve your work – you will discover tools to help you renegotiate and improve your present job or create opportunities where you are now.

For those of you who like to focus on getting results or want to act quickly, there is a great deal of *how to*. The advice offered here also takes account of the rapid changes in the world of work which happened during 2020, with new tactics on offer to match new conditions.

The book's title isn't misleading – it's written to help you reflect *and* act. To write it, I've drawn on decades of experience. Some of this has been spent training interviewers and recruiters. The rest has been spent working as a career coach – in contexts ranging from community job clubs to executive career changers.

The book is stuffed with practical tips to help you avoid the obvious mistakes people make when job hunting. I've included every short cut I can think of, especially techniques that increase your chances of getting short-listed. I've included interview tips, insights into negotiating a job offer, and methods of reaching people when face-to-face contact is tricky.

How to use this book

This book is designed to be a complete career change programme in one volume. You may read it in a couple of days, or even in a few hours. For some of you it will feel like an unfolding conversation, a time to think, learn, and try things out.

If you find yourself thinking *I don't have time for all this*, think again. You are considering your career, not choosing your next smartphone or a holiday destination. Work absorbs time in those decades of your life where you have most stamina and energy. It consumes a great deal of who you are. The decisions prompted by this book can easily impact your work for decades ahead. So, make time – invest time in your future.

You don't have to read this book front to back like a novel. Jump to sections which look interesting, exercises that speak to you right now, or tips you need most urgently. Look at the chapter headings and plan your way through the material. Try to find time to come back to the sections on self-discovery and new thinking, because ultimately this is where you find tips to help you get better results from time invested, and avoid rookie mistakes.

You may find that a single exercise unlocks your potential, or you may gain multiple insights from using several ideas or exercises. One word of advice: if the exercise doesn't work for you, don't feel you have 'failed'. All it means is this: *the exercise doesn't work for you.* Put it aside and move on.

Downloadable exercises

If you're reading this as an e-book, don't get frustrated if you feel you can't complete the exercises easily. Many can be completed by simply using a notebook, but for those exercises with boxes to complete, A4 copies are available for **download** free of charge (see the members' section of www.johnleescareers.com).

Maps for the journey ahead

The opening chapters of this book focus on the way we think about work following the mind-bending changes of 2020. Chapter 2 takes a hard look at what gets in the way of finding satisfying work, including psychological barriers to change. Chapters 3 and 4 invite you to take control of your career by thinking of it as a healthy compromise between your personal drivers and what the market has to offer, revealing some new tools for planning and decision-making. Chapter 5 is titled **Thinking, deciding, and getting on**

with it, and does what it says on the tin – kick-starting your creative thinking, then turning from reflection to action.

Chapters 6–9 offer you the chance to understand yourself better – by exploring your **career hot buttons**, your hidden and motivated **skills**, your chosen areas of **knowledge**, and the key aspects of **personality** that will shape your career, including an overview of your **values**.

If you're wondering how to choose a career and work that feel worth doing, read Chapter 10 on choosing work sectors, and Chapter 11 on changing to a career path where work is more interesting or purposeful, possibly closer to a calling.

Chapter 11 also gives you the opportunity to take an exciting free **online Career Change Test from Careershifters** (see p. 147).

The first half of the book explores the work that suits you best and how to decide on a direction of travel. Chapters 12–16 give you practical advice on finding a great job, with strategies in Chapter 12 on **smarter job searching** and in-depth discussion of the **hidden job market**. Chapter 13 shows how to operate **online** and manage your social media impact, and Chapter 14 reveals how career breakthroughs often happen through different kinds of conversations, ranging from simple encouragement to structured information interviews using the REVEAL method.

Under time pressure to get interviews quickly? Chapter 15 offers a **4-hour job search programme** (new in this edition), showing you how to make best use of your time and achieve quick results. Chapter 16 offers concise help on sharpening up your **interview technique**.

Check out Chapter 17 on the range of working models you might consider, including **portfolio careers**. Chapter 18 is written specially for those **moving into work after leaving full-time education**, including school leavers.

Once you have completed this central section of the book, you will be ready to complete the **Master Sheet** (p. 261).

Appendix 2 contains **CV and cover letter tips**, with examples. Appendix 3 outlines a range of **case studies** – people who have changed their careers using this book.

Guest contributors

In this book, you will find not only my own views but advice from a wide range of experts:

- Richard Alderson on Shift Projects (Chapter 4)
- Peter Fennah on personality tests and assessment events (Chapter 9)
- Joëlle Warren on working with executive recruiters (Chapter 12)
- Julian Childs, Matthias Feist, and Ruth Winden on getting the best out of the internet and social media (Chapter 13)
- Kate Howlett on interview tips (Chapter 16)

New in this edition

Every edition involves extensive revisions and updates, and this is no exception. Most chapters have been rewritten extensively. The book contains up-to-date research and insights into the jobs market, a strategy for career success at a time of job fragility, and deeper insights into the way fewer jobs are advertised and more roles go 'underground'. The book continues to provide support for everyone asking the question, 'what kind of career would suit me best?'

New features

- An overview of **Shift Projects** (Chapter 4).
- A link to a free Careershifters online **Career Change Test** (see p. 147).

- Insights into the **current job market** – continuing job fragility, insecurity, 'good work', managing your career in a flat organisation.
- New material on **working purposefully**, perhaps with a sense of calling (Chapter 11).
- Updated material on managing your **social media presence** (Chapter 13).
- Updated material on what will **shorten your job search**.
- Effective strategies to help with the unadvertised, **hidden job market**.
- A brand new section offering a **240-minute job search in 7 Steps** (Chapter 15).

New exercises

- **Career Transition Diamonds**, with new thinking on career experimentation and early action (Chapter 4).
- A revised **values** exercise (Chapter 9).
- Revised exercises on discovering new **sectors** and combining work ideas (Chapter 10).
- **Getting Your Story in Focus** – a new exercise on storytelling your way into a new kind of work (Chapter 11).
- A checklist to assess your **Market Readiness** (Chapter 15).

'Get a job you love?'
Get real . . .

'There is no point in work unless it absorbs you
like an absorbing game'.

D.H. Lawrence

This chapter helps you to:

- Gain insights into a rapidly changing job market
- Understand employment fragility
- Learn how job hunting has altered dramatically
- Understand how to start to be in control of your career
- Move out of passive, 'default' mode

Work in a changing world

This book looks at the way work fits into our lives, and whether we can hope to be happy in it. I have had the interesting experience of standing next to someone picking up this book in a bookshop. If they're with a friend, they often read the title out. I'm always interested to hear the reply. It will be anything from 'sounds interesting' to a cynical 'hmmm . . . *I wish*'.

Publishing a book titled *How to Get a Job You Love* every 2 years for over two decades has required more than a little nerve in terms of the ups and downs of the job market. As we enter the third decade of the 21st Century, gradually rebuilding after the year of the great shutdown, working life is going through the biggest change for several generations.

In early 2020 we were still rebalancing after the period of turbulence beginning in 2008, the 'great recession'. Just as we were emerging from those troubled times, Brexit and uncertainties about international trade deals placed more clouds on the horizon. That was all, of course, before the life-changing events of 2020.

In the opening weeks of 2020, the UK economy was buoyant. In the three months to February 2020 the Office for National Statistics recorded a record-breaking 33.1 million people in work, 352,000 more than a year earlier. In the winter of 2019/2020, the number of self-employed people exceeded 5 million for the first time.

With unemployment low, employers complained of skill shortages. A CIPD/Adecco report recorded '67% of organisations' experiencing 'hard-to-fill vacancies'. The Recruitment and Employment Confederation reported (2020) that the UK's recruitment industry was turning over £38.9 billion annually, placing over a million people in permanent roles, and a slightly higher number of temporary workers.

Employment figures after April 2020 tell a different story. In April, 140,000 UK employers applied for help to pay wage bills through the government's job retention scheme, funding 80% of furloughed workers' wages. Over 1.8 million people made new benefits claims in the 6 weeks to April 12, 2020. In the USA, 3 million new claims for unemployment benefit were filed in one week in March.

The economic impact of 2020 has yet to be measured. Many businesses quietly ceased trading. Some commentators predicted unemployment levels not seen since the 1930s. Fortunately there are signs of re-emergence as governments across the world invest to protect and create jobs. Economies will recover, but are unlikely to look the same.

As we emerge from this unprecedented crisis, where next for work?

Job Fragility

Even before the disruptions of 2020, a significant portion of the workforce had a feeling that their job might be restructured, changed, or disappear completely. This sense of job fragility will continue as we emerge from the downturn, because we will be in recovery mode for quite some time.

Jobs will continue to be transient – or feel as if they are. The market will no doubt experience further changes in workforce numbers, with companies swinging rapidly from further cutbacks to new hiring programmes. Skill shortages may still exist, giving some candidates market leverage. Many will find themselves in continuing uncertainty, perhaps having to apply for internal roles to avoid redundancy, or look outside for alternative employment.

When organisations reinvent themselves several times a decade, and when markets are deeply uncertain, employers play it safe. This can mean an increase in fixed-term contracts and interim appointments to avoid adding to the headcount. Selection processes are often extended and have more stages. Risk-averse managers require candidates to attend four or more selection events and wait an extraordinarily long time for a decision. Commonly organisations rethink half way through a hiring process, either reconsidering the role or taking it off the table. Such decisions have little to do with the quality of candidates, but experiences like this can easily dampen confidence.

Where organisations have restructured extensively, the psychological contract has clearly been weakened, if not torn up. This is most obvious where staff have to apply for their own jobs, or have to perform work previously done by two workers. A research study (de Jong et al, 2016) revealed that when organisations restructure, there is a measurably negative effect on employee well-being – even where there are no job losses. This has inevitable implications for engagement and loyalty.

We all know people affected by redundancy. Widespread redundancies at least have a positive side: employers see many candidates who at some point in their career have been 'let go'; the stigma of redundancy is lessened (however, the issue still needs handling carefully in interviews).

From hero to zero

Many jobs created after 2008 were low-paid and sometimes low skill, with limited prospects for development or advancement. Those in these kinds of jobs felt the impact of the COVID-19 crisis more acutely, but uncertainty was also magnified for those workers furloughed, unsure whether their jobs would still exist after the lockdown. Those with few qualifications, or in casual jobs, were most impacted.

At the start of 2020, over 850,000 people were working on zero-hours contracts, where employers avoid any commitments to working hours. Some people take on more than one job when working hours are not guaranteed. For employers, the practice offers flexibility, but most zero-hours workers surveyed say they would prefer predictable hours and income. There are implications for informal staff development. When workers are sent home at quiet times, they can miss out on useful learning in quieter moments where staff re-organise, plan, and learn to get on with each other better.

Workers of all ages expressed concerns about job security even before 2020, and the jobs market has been tough on workers over 50. However, the biggest impact seems to be on younger workers. The Resolution Foundation (2018) outlined the challenges faced by young workers in the UK, stating that it will be years before we understand the real impact on pay and career progression of 'insecure and low paid work'.

What career path?

In recent decades organisations have become flatter and leaner. Whole tiers of management have been removed, and workers are expected to cover a wider range of tasks. The lack of obvious pathways for promotion can be disorienting for younger workers who passively expect to be groomed for senior roles, and others who buy into unsupportable employer branding. In flat organisations, individuals have to make lateral moves to advance, or go elsewhere. Such moves often require highly developed relationship-building and networking skills. A lack of promotion opportunities and job security prompts some to consider alternative options, including portfolio careers (see Chapter 17).

Today's workplace can lead to new variations on FOMO (fear of missing out) – do you jump ship or wait to be recognised? Career decision-making has become more complex, especially the classic question 'do I go or do I stay?' Some change roles because of a lack of a pay rise or promotion, but with an unclear sense of what they're moving into. Those who stay passively sit and wait for a tap on the shoulder that never comes. Even in a tight market some people look on the bright side, saying, 'if I'm going to lose my job, I might as well find something interesting'. Others feel their options are narrow and they will take anything; they quickly discover that this undifferentiated message makes them singularly unattractive to employers.

New working relationships

Where does this extraordinary volatility leave organisations trying to manage talent – and individuals managing their careers? The planning horizon for organisations is now much closer than it was ten years ago. If you don't know what kind of business you'll be in six months' time, how do you recruit for the long term? Employers make promises to talent, but these are frequently put aside. Organisations are having to reinvent themselves on the hoof. They still have highly developed 'employer brands' to attract new staff, but employers will probably have to change the script in terms of promises made about developing and keeping their best people.

In the past organisations took pride in offering career futures – promotion ladders, development opportunities designed to assure workers that they would be retained and valued. Even in early 2020 hirers were unable to offer career pathways extending much beyond three to five years. Employers may have to be much more transparent about what they can really offer – something closer to a work *project*. This will still be a valuable block of experience, but with an expiry date. Soon, the idea of long-term talent retention may seem like an antiquated, old-century idea. Employers still have a great deal to offer: useful experience, intensive skill development, job and sector knowledge, and the chance to work with exciting people, brands, and technology.

When short-term fix becomes the new normal

Even though there is huge pressure for society to return to business as usual following lockdown, some assumptions and habits may have adjusted forever. A 'return to normal' will be a new normal. Perhaps the most obvious example is a complete shift in thinking around distance and home working. Before COVID-19 this was largely prompted by worker lifestyle choice. In the lockdown many staff had no option but to work from home, rapidly learning to use Zoom, Skype, or similar technologies, to be managed from a distance, and to self-motivate in terms of pace of work. In the space of a fortnight motorways became quiet and skies empty, and across the world, work was devolved to homes.

This international home working experiment will probably change work forever. As economies revive, there will of course be incentives encouraging business travel, but every institution, from parliament to small community groups, has learned to work at a distance, and with vastly reduced meeting costs. Organisations who have felt the pain of maintaining largely functionless office space will no doubt reflect on the advantages of virtual work. It seems likely that some will want to continue working this way – especially if commuting seems an expensive distraction from productivity.

Work will continue to change fast in other ways. Unprecedented funding into healthcare, pharmaceuticals and IT brings surprising possibilities. Technology will continue to become faster and cheaper, opening up new markets and working methods. The video conferencing tools we use today will soon be considered antiquated and unresponsive, replaced by software which more authentically replicates real meetings and conversations.

Operating on auto-pilot

When the rules of the game change every year, we all need to have more control of our careers. Many people are passive about career decisions, leaving job satisfaction very much to chance. They talk about being flattered or pushed into jobs, and they talk about where they have 'ended up'.

Job fragility sometimes persuades workers to keep their head down, cruise on auto-pilot for a while, and put career development on hold. The flaw in this strategy is clear when you explain your CV in a job interview, where you may struggle to prove that your skills are up to date. If your CV suggests you've spent some time soft-pedalling, now might be the right time to gain new experience. You can do other things too, such as learning to present your career story as a coherent narrative, a series of conscious choices ('I decided it would be better to remain in the role and see how I could develop it . . .').

Passive thinking allows life to go on around us. It's easy to shrug off responsibility with a phrase like *A job's a job. It pays the bills. Jobs are hard to find.* New occupations are opening up all the time, and people are sampling a broad range of them during the course of a working lifetime. Pension insecurity means we are working later in life, but this gives us broader scope for career refreshment.

When you're trying to reposition yourself in the job market, two things really help: optimism and curiosity. Optimistic thinking keeps the end in mind, encouraging you to keep pushing on doors, asking questions. Curiosity compels you to do so. Both radiate energy. And that's a great starting point for finding a job you love. You will need energy to fuel what might be a long slog of exploration, but energy, enthusiasm, evident motivation, and a real interest in some aspect of work – these are things that make sure you're remembered. Attitude and positive thinking need to be backed up with personal evidence. This is the practical, vital matter of expertly matching yourself to employer needs, a major theme in this book.

Conventional job searching (see Chapter 12 on unconventional methods) means you pretty much guarantee you will hear radio silence. That's the most commonly experienced market response – nothing. Attractive advertised positions are known in the recruitment industry as 'candidate magnets'. Chasing them often means a lot of effort with zero return. Many employers freely acknowledge that they don't respond to job applications unless they are inviting candidates to interview.

Job hunting – a game with new rules

In a typical year one in ten people change jobs – that's in addition to people entering work for the first time. Sometimes job mobility is forced on workers; at other times it seems an attractive option. Job confidence can be measured by the numbers who choose to resign from a job in order to take up another. This benchmark is what FT journalist Sarah O'Connor (2015) calls the 'Take This Job and Shove It Index' – looking at the number of people who resign voluntarily in order to take up a more attractive role.

Deep insecurity in employment leaves people feeling there are fewer opportunities than there used to be. This will be true for a while. The rules of the game change considerably in periods of higher unemployment. We saw something of this in the recession which began in 2008, and the picture from 2020 onwards is more acute. When jobs are in short supply, a buyer's market follows. Organisations offer less, and ask more, and it can be harder to find satisfying work.

However, there is still a great deal of movement and activity; the difference is these movements are often unseen – we're often unaware of vacancies until they are filled. Also, new *types* of jobs are invented all the time.

Something interesting has happened in the world of work. Looking back over the 20-plus years of this book's lifetime, job hunting has changed dramatically. Until the early part of this century, jobs were much more visible. Many of them were advertised – obvious targets for job seekers, involving a relatively straightforward application process.

Recent recessions have deepened a trend that began earlier in the century. Jobs have gone under the radar; only a small proportion are advertised conventionally. Employers have learned many cheap and smart ways of attracting talent. Sometimes this is high-tech (for example, attracting and enlisting crowds of would-be workers to websites). Others use a canny mix of social media, organisational job boards, and word of mouth. In today's marketplace, jobs are increasingly filled by low-cost, low-visibility, informal methods. This is the 'hidden' job market, which seems to get bigger every year (see Chapter 12).

Looking for a job effectively means spending less time on internet searching and form-filling, and more on conversations and connections – highly developed soft skills. If this seems outside your capability, don't despair. This book outlines the easiest ways of doing this, short cuts, and workarounds for those looking for alternatives to face-to-face networking.

When most jobs were visible, even relatively passive job seekers usually found something, sometimes just as a result of bulk applications. If you judge the state of the jobs market by the number of advertised positions available, you'll feel rather despondent. Compared with just ten years ago, a huge amount of responsibility has transferred to individuals in terms of shaping their future.

New graduates often complain that job hunting looks like a rather low-skill chore. Surely writing a CV isn't rocket science, and applying for jobs is just about uploading your CV? Many job hunters believe that looking for a job is as straightforward as opening a new account with an online retailer – a simple matter of entering data onto screens. The reality is rather different. Today, looking for a new role (particularly a senior job, a creative job, or a job in a niche or new sector) requires sophisticated skills – influencing, connecting, communicating, savvy use of social media, and the ability to build relationships quickly. The process is less like form-filling and more like *trying to get elected to public office*.

You need a clear message, and you need to know how to get it across. You need to influence key decision-makers, followers, ambassadors, and champions. Most of all, you need to learn how to be visible – so *jobs find you*. It's not simply about completing online forms and pressing 'enter' – it's a complex task requiring high-level skills.

Reframing

However long it takes for the economy to turn around, you'll need resilience to cope with the roller-coaster ride of job hunting. It helps by adopting some of the techniques taught to us by positive psychology. For example, focusing on helpful and constructive feedback on your CV and LinkedIn profile, rather than jumping to conclusions when an employer fails to acknowledge an application or a recruiter fails to return your call.

A great deal of this is about *reframing*. Focus on what's working in your job searching rather than what isn't. Since you need to be open to new ideas, challenge assumptions that get in the way – see Chapter 2 for barriers and Chapter 12 for market myths. Watch out for limitations you put in your own way – favourite internal scripts like 'it's all about who you know. . .'. Look closely at these scripts in your personal soap opera. Examine the way you think about opportunity, luck, and change. Do you see closed doors, or doors with handles?

Ah, that depends . . . And it does. It depends *how you look*. Look for possibilities, not barriers. Don't assume the answer will be 'no' before you ask the question. Look at the number of times you receive praise each day and ignore it. How many times do you hear neutral or objective data and take it the wrong way? How often do you hear criticism and clutch it to yourself as the last, final, and totally accurate picture of *you*? Human beings find it easy to ignore positive information, and distort neutral information into something negative.

Some people find interesting and well-paid work even when opportunities seem to be thin on the ground. Are they lucky? To a small extent. The rest is down to how they choose to think, and how they choose to act.

Exercise 1.1 – Breaking out of default mode

Electronic devices have a 'default mode', often the original factory settings. When you're looking for a new job, employers, recruiters, and other contacts make assumptions about what you're looking for. For example, recruitment agencies may assume you want a similar role to the one you held most recently.

Think about the 'default mode' your career suggests, using the prompts below.

	What role will people expect you to undertake next in 'default mode' . . .
Based on your last job?	
Based on your career history?	
Based on page 1 of your CV?	
Based on your LinkedIn profile?	
Based on your most recent qualifications or training?	

What would you really like to do? What would you call that job?

If you can't name the job, how is it different from the 'default' jobs listed above?

'Must do' list

- ✓ Use a good quality notebook to jot down your discoveries and the results of the exercises in this book. Write down the steps you need to take in the next two months. Then take step one.
- ✓ Plan ahead. Look at the chapter headings and decide how and when you are going to set aside time to go through this process. If time is pressing, go to Chapter 15.
- ✓ Reflect: have your career decisions been made consciously, or have you largely responded to opportunity and chance? How much of your career is about regret or missed opportunity?
- ✓ What's the 'default' mode for your career? What will happen if you do nothing?
- ✓ Look again at your experiences of applying for jobs. What's working well for you? What could you do differently?
- ✓ Identify someone you know who has very clearly taken control of their career. Find out their first steps, how they made change happen, and how they sustain their energy.

2

Barriers and blocks

'What work I have done I have done because it has been play.
If it had been work I shouldn't have done it'.

Mark Twain

This chapter explores the following topics:

- The mindset that helps you avoid change
- The blocks between you and a great career
- Overcoming personal barriers
- Defining your preferred time balance in a job.

Dealing with 'yes, but'

At this point, you may be hearing two familiar words in your head: **'yes, but . . .'**. We all do it. It's your ancient brain speaking – the part attuned to avoiding risk and seeking safety. It's the senior committee member who faithfully attends every meeting in your brain and says: 'We've heard all this stuff before', 'It'll never fly', 'It might work for somebody more talented', or 'It might work in London'.

'Yes, but' thinking is the biggest block to career transition. Saying 'yes, but' is a good way of avoiding change: 'Yes, but I have to earn a living', 'Yes, but in the real world . . .'. It's often a sign that the speaker isn't listening positively – it's a classic defence mechanism, a way of avoiding even thinking about change. 'Yes, but' allows you to pretend that you're making a sensible decision by avoiding risk. You'll justify it using all the old phrases: 'The grass is always greener . . .', 'Better the devil you know . . .'.

What's really limiting about this thinking is that it stops you in your tracks. 'Yes, but' thinking gives you plenty of logical, safety-first reasons to do nothing at all.

The biggest and most important decision facing you right now isn't about changing jobs. It's about taking just

Exercise 2.1 – Constraints

We all have constraints, but each of us thinks that our constraints are uniquely limiting. Tick the constraints that you feel apply to you.

☐ I am too old	☐ I don't have many achieve-
☐ I am under-qualified	ments
☐ My experience is all in one industry	☐ I worry about taking risks
☐ I have a health problem	☐ Don't know what I want to do next
☐ Location	☐ Worry that I will be out of
☐ Travel	work for a long time
☐ Lack of information about the job market	☐ Fear of employer's attitude to redundancy
☐ The stigma of unemployment	☐ Lack of up-to-date skills
☐ Financial commitments	☐ Fear of rejection
☐ Family/personal problems	☐ Lack of relevant qualifications
☐ Fear of approaching people	☐ Worry about having to retrain/
☐ Lack of confidence selling myself in person	go back to full-time study
☐ My job search to date hasn't worked	☐ I want a job that looks good on my CV
☐ Don't want to make the wrong decision at my time of life	☐ I have never had to apply for a job before
	☐ I don't interview well

one small step of discovery. One phone call. One email. One face-to-face conversation focused on finding out what's out there. The 'yes, but' mindset is locked down. It stops you in your tracks, ensuring that you fail before you try anything. Your 'yes, but' brain thinks it's avoiding a risky, big step. The end result is this: you avoid taking any steps at all.

You don't have to make a radical change overnight. In fact, you don't need to make any kind of big decision right now. You just need to decide to take one small decision: to *look*. To find out, ask questions, follow your curiosity.

Look at the Constraints exercise above, and think about the items you've ticked. Highlight the top half dozen which limit you most. When have you overcome them in the past? How?

Look at the constraints you have little control over – for example, travel-to-work distance or working hours. Knowing which constraints seem to be fixed can be helpful. Some constraints simply describe learning needs: 'I don't interview well' means it's time for more practice.

Psychological constraints are the most powerful, such as 'I don't want to make the wrong decision at my time of life'. These thoughts limit your performance – one-liners that pop into your head when you consider risk.

Personal barriers, and creative ways to overcome them

Fear of making mistakes. The world's greatest inventions are the result of mistakes. Mistakes are simply feedback on our performance. Winners make far more mistakes than losers – they get more feedback as they continue to try out more possibilities. The timid mind stops after one mistake. Try a trial-and-error approach – 'doubling your failure rate'.

Rejection dampens confidence. In a job search you will be rejected more times than you are accepted. This is a statistical fact, not a reflection of what you have to offer. Plan for rejection. Learn from each application, then move on. The brain likes to linger on negative thoughts and we need ways of maintaining confidence. US President Abraham Lincoln carried with him a newspaper clipping stating that he was a great leader. John Lennon's school report suggested he was on the road to failure. We all need a little more encouragement.

I don't know if I want the job. Research, and find out. Compare your 'I wish' list to the employer's 'We want' list. If you find a reasonable overlap, throw yourself at the opportunity with enthusiasm. If there are difficult decisions to make about location, working hours, or pay, don't worry about them until the job offer is actually in your hand.

I don't like talking about my strengths. Some people find it embarrassing to talk about what they do well. In some cultures, the idea of the 'tall poppy' means that people avoid being seen as distinctive or having particular achievements. Recognise your achievements and find your authentic voice so you can talk about where you can make an important contribution.

No clear direction. You might assume that you can't begin working on your career without knowing where you're going. Set out to discover options, and leave big decisions until you have a lot more data. Don't apologise for being uncertain what you're looking for; talk about enjoying the process of exploring. Find the right audiences: employers and recruitment consultants are put off by uncertainty.

Image. Find out how others see you. When you practise interview skills, ask for feedback on your body language and dress sense.

Handling the shock of the new. Remember times when you made significant changes. How long was your adjustment period? You are probably better at adjusting to new than you believe. Even the most demanding environment can become familiar and routine within a matter of months.

The expectations of others. Don't let other people live your career for you. Everyone does it: family, friends, teachers, colleagues. They paint a picture of the future (based on scant information) and you feel obliged to live it out. Find people who can give you objective information about how the world of work is changing.

How other people push you up and down. Watch for *drains* and *radiators*. Some people are drains: they not only react negatively to your ideas but also absorb your energy. You seem to spend a lot of time managing their pessimism. Others are more like *radiators*. They push energy out, encouraging and inspiring. Radiators will say 'go for it'. Drains say 'that will never work'. Drains tell you to be 'realistic', which usually means doing next to nothing in the hope that something else will come along.

I can't get on with it . . . Start with small goals – and stick to them. Plan your week ahead: find someone to take out for coffee so you can explore ideas and start to practise talking about your work history.

Protect your ideas. New ideas need nurturing. Sometimes the worst thing you can do is to share them with the wrong kind of people and have them dismissed or trashed. Share ideas for exploration with positive-minded people.

Watch your **energy levels.** As you begin exploring, your enthusiasm is high. It can easily flag – often when you hit the first obstacle. Plan *now* to talk to someone positive at that critical time. Get other people to make you accountable for your short-term goals.

It's a dog-eat-dog world. Don't make the mistake of thinking you're in competition with everyone else. You're not. You're up against the requirements of specific jobs and the needs of particular employers.

Problems for the career doctor

Time to discuss your various 'yes, but' symptoms. The career doctor will see you now.

The jobs aren't there

Finding a job you love for at least half the week can seem hard if you aren't seeing vacancies. As Chapters 1 and 12 reveal, jobs are increasingly off-radar. Every day people leave jobs or retire and new roles are created. Exciting roles can even be found when employers don't seem to be hiring. What's important is this: *the economy isn't in your head*. If it dictates every choice, every action, your reaction to every opportunity, then you're buying in to the majority view that it's not worth exploring.

Too long in the same job

The 'same job' could have been a 20-year history of change, variety, and development. We're not demotivated by being in one job or one organisation. We're turned off when things start repeating themselves and we're not learning or changing. Even if you're in a great job that you love doing, you may not want to do it forever. Most careers need a reboot from time to time.

The side benefits are good

In one firm, an employee stayed on for several years because somebody brought in cake every day. We all have our reasons for avoiding change. If you find yourself saying, 'The pension scheme / the medical insurance / the gym is so good . . .', then the question should be: *but is this why I'm here?* Side benefits evaporate quickly when organisations cut costs. When your last day on earth arrives, are you going to say, 'I wish my pension had been just a bit bigger' or 'Why did I waste 20 years in that office watching the clock?'

I'll stick at it

'The job's okay, and a lot of things are good about it, and even though it's boring, it's a good place to ride out the storm . . .'. There are a lot of people in the workplace today who think that way. The problem is that dull jobs create dull people. Once a job is no longer challenging, you've made a strange pact with yourself: *I will trade boredom for security*. This will mean future problems explaining your CV choices.

I'll never earn what I earn here

This one's the kiss of death, because it's really saying, 'I'm overpaid here, and no other employer will let me get away with it'. This is usually wrong-headed. Few people stay overpaid for long. If you're making a big hole in the payroll and not delivering much in return, this is a good time to rethink.

I don't want to make the wrong decision

Hoping for a low-risk career, a job that will take you safely through to retirement, is a hopeless longing for work to be like it was at some mythical time in the past. We have to take career decisions for ourselves, and the fear of getting them wrong can be disabling. Being motivated to *avoid* danger can mean that your energy goes into avoiding the first steps of exploration. Incremental thinking only gets you incremental results. Change happens when you do at least one thing differently.

I just need a job

You may by now be thinking that this advice is for other people, not you. You feel you need something that pays the bills, right now. This makes you vulnerable in the labour market. It may persuade you to become a 'job beggar', with your hat in your hand, saying, 'I'll do anything'.

That's a great way to avoid being hired. Some years ago I worked with a group of job seekers in a Johannesburg township. One of them, Gugu, was aged 17 and had given up looking for work. Why? 'There are no jobs in South Africa', she said. I pointed out that new jobs were being created in that country every day. 'Yes, but so many people are chasing them', she said sadly. Talking to her I realised that all over the world too many people fall into job-beggar mode. Fortunately, Gugu and her fellow job seekers all found jobs – as a result of a programme encouraging them to find confidence talking about their abilities and experience.

No, it's true: I just need a job

Perhaps an inner voice is saying, 'get *real* – looking for an enjoyable job is self-indulgence, a daydream'. How many excuses do you need to have to ensure you stay miserable at work? Listen to successful people talking about the work they do. They don't often say, 'Well, the money's good'. They talk about work being like a 'game', or they talk about doing work they would gladly do for nothing.

When jobs are thin on the ground, you might also think, '*there are no choices*'. Just get some perspective on that statement. Compared with most of the world's population, past and present, people in today's developed world have a huge range of life choices, and more protection against failure. We all have choices. Some people find brilliant jobs even in the depths of a recession. In February 2020, just before the lockdown, more people were employed in the UK than at any time in its history, yet you could still hear people saying, 'This is a really bad time to be looking for a new job'. If you take the first thing that comes along, how are you going to explain that when your CV is scrutinised in years to come?

Effective career planning is about finding a job that works for you, matching who you are to the life you are going to lead. That's not a luxury, not a fantasy: it's your choice of reality.

I'm too old

Yes, employers are wrong-headed about age and often assume that younger people are more adaptable and have more stamina. You can easily find organisations that are evidently 'young' cultures, where it can be hard for older workers to break in. Some employers do of course have an unenlightened view of older workers, who can of course offer important characteristics – commitment, wisdom, common sense, and reliability.

Age matters if you draw attention to it. Emphasise that you're a great fit for the job and an experienced, safe pair of hands. In your CV, minimise details about jobs you did more than 20 years ago. At interview don't talk about how things 'used to be done' or confess that you find modern technology or social media mystifying.

Employers who discriminate on the grounds of age are either too young to appreciate that anyone can have an original idea over the age of 30 (so show them . . .) or old and tired and assume that everyone over 40 is equally old and tired. If the employer wants a 20-year-old to burnout in 18 months, do you want to be there anyway?

I don't have the qualifications

Formal qualifications are often less relevant than people think. There are so many degrees, diplomas, and certificates that employers can't tell one from another, and they have little idea if any predict workplace performance.

In the (rarer than you might think) event that a particular qualification is a stated requirement, then ask yourself, 'why do they need this? – what problem will it solve?' For many roles, relevant experience is often an acceptable alternative. Talk about what you know and what you can do: make your answers specific to the problems posed in this job.

I don't have the money to retrain

Almost every journalist seeking career change tips asks, 'Don't people have to retrain?' Most of us assume that career change means full-time learning. Look for alternative ways in. Don't let 'I'd need to retrain' become a job myth that stops you finding out. Is there something you can learn in your own time? If you think you need a specific qualification, find out if it will improve your employability or just put a hole in your bank balance.

I don't really understand 'online'

At one time using a computer was considered a specialised skill. Now under-fives do it. It's not rocket science. If you claim proudly that you don't use social media, employers assume you don't care about the way work is done today. Get connected, and check your email at least once a day.

There are a million things the web makes easier: research, finding people to speak to, discovering new ideas, tracking down former colleagues, seeking recommendations and endorsements. Trying to achieve these outcomes without using the internet is rather like trying to cook a three-course meal over a candle flame – an unnecessary challenge providing indifferent results very, *very* slowly.

I might be found out

It's surprising how many senior staff share a common fear: *one day I'll be found out*. This is the **impostor syndrome**, first recognised in the 1970s, and widely experienced. Many people believe they got a job through luck and they are fakes. Their secret fear is that one day their boss will say, 'Okay, we know it's been a big pretence. Just leave now and we'll say nothing more about it'. A worrying number of people would leave the building without protest.

Insecurity is everywhere. The strange thing is that most workers assume that top-level bosses are immune to it. In fact, many senior staff are so isolated they spend more energy than anyone else coping with feeling like an impostor.

I don't interview well

Absolute statements like this set you up to fail. Start with small steps: catalogue what you've done and learn how to talk about it. Read Chapter 16.

I can't summon up the energy to change career

If you're in work that no longer floats your boat, it's easy to feel the only solution is job change. This may be an unfounded assumption. Review your current job and ask yourself what you would like to change. Is it the role, the people around you, the organisation, or something else? What parts of the job make the time pass quickly?

Make a list, then be clear about what you can change, and what you can't. Ask for a career conversation. Retaining people is much cheaper than hiring new staff, and you may get better results fixing the job you are in rather than going to the market to find a new one. Use Exercise 2.2 to understand how your time is spent, and what you'd like to change. What activities would you like to increase or decrease? What difference would that make to your effectiveness?

Exercise 2.2 – Time balance

How would you like to spend your time at work? What would be the ideal time balance?

Think about your current or most recent job. In the left-hand column, estimate the percentage of time you spend in each kind of activity. In the right-hand column, state your preferred time allocation, again as a percentage. Each column should add up to 100.

Actual %	Activity	Preferred %
	Working entirely alone Working on my own without distraction. Working things out, being given space to sort out a problem or finish a piece of work, writing something, having time to reflect . . .	
	Working independently but close to colleagues Being responsible for own results but having colleagues around. Having ready access to the ideas and encouragement of other people . . .	
	Working 1:1 Explaining, persuading, influencing, selling, coaching, managing, teaching . . .	

	Attending meetings Meeting to deal with agendas, share information, and make collective decisions	
	Working in active teams Group problem-solving, planning, brainstorming, reviewing, getting things done, training, motivating . . .	
	Extending your network Telephoning new contacts, networking, meeting plenty of new people, going to conferences, seminars . . .	
	Working with an audience Public speaking, performing, entertaining, giving talks, informing larger groups . . .	
100%	Total	**100%**

When you have completed the time balance exercise, compare your current role with your ideal. This isn't self-indulgence or fantasy – it's a healthy recognition of how you work at your best. Look at the activities where you spend most of your time. Which would you like to increase or decrease, substantially? What difference would that make to your effectiveness?

'Must do' list

- ✓ Career problems are sometimes concrete, but usually strategies for avoiding change. What are your favourite 'yes, but' defences?
- ✓ Look at your constraints, particularly the ones that get in the way of making progress.
- ✓ You can be happy at work. What first step could you take to achieve that? How would your friends and colleagues notice the difference?
- ✓ Look at your CV, your interview style, your attitude to work. You complain that employers see negative things about you. How many of these messages are actually composed and delivered by you? How can you reframe the way you present yourself?
- ✓ Use the time balance exercise to get a broad picture of what your ideal job would look like in terms of activities.

Getting more out of work

'No small misery is caused by overworked and unhappy people,
in the dark views which they necessarily take up themselves,
and force upon others, of work itself'.

John Ruskin

This chapter helps you to:

- Look at what you get out of work
- Look at what work takes out of you
- Reflect on your work satisfaction – and how you can improve it
- Start to define work that feels more interesting and stimulating
- Assemble your jigsaw job.

The good, the bad, and the just plain awful

The word 'career' comes from the Latin *carrus*, a wheeled vehicle (linked to 'chariot' or 'carriage'). In other words, it's a vehicle that takes us through life. Another use of the word is *to move in an uncontrolled direction*, as in 'The steering failed, and my car careered across the motorway'. Random movement in an uncontrolled direction. Does that sound familiar?

A great deal of research has been undertaken in the last two decades on worker engagement. It seems that only a small proportion of employees feel committed to their work, and many are likely to leave the job if another opportunity presents itself. On the other hand, engaged workers often say they would continue in the same job if they had a multi-million lottery win. Clearly, work motivation is a complicated arena.

Exercise 3.1 – How happy are you in your work?

Tick the box next to the description which best describes your work right now.

☐ **Great job**

I often feel I can't wait to get into work. Work is the place where I grow and learn most, where I am set healthy challenges, where I am valued and appreciated. A great deal of fun and self-esteem is centred in my work, which fits my values, talents, and personality. I know that I make a difference. I express who I am in my job. The rewards are right, and I would be happy to be paid less if necessary. I love the part work plays in my life.

☐ **Thumbs up**

I enjoy work most of the time, but sometimes there are headaches and problems. My work feels useful and contributes to my self-esteem. My contribution is clear, acknowledged, and significant. My career is a good match to my talents, personality, and values. I am appreciated by others. I feel that I make a difference, and that I add something positive to the organisation. I find supervision helpful, but my boss is more a mentor than a supervisor. I lead a satisfying career which contributes to all parts of my life.

☐ **Mustn't grumble**

I accept the work I do. Sometimes I feel valued, other times exploited or ignored. Work is stable, largely unexciting, doesn't interfere with my inner life too much. New ways of doing things are sometimes discouraged. I may be in the right line of work, but in the wrong organisation. I am valued for some of what I do, but not always the most important things.

☐ **Someone's got to do it**

I work because I need to. I don't feel I owe a great deal to my employer. Several parts of the job are unpleasant/boring/demeaning/pointless. Real life begins at five o'clock. I'm not learning anything. I try to make a contribution but sometimes hit a brick wall. My skills are getting rusty. I would just like a quiet life.

☐ **Clock watcher**

There are days I almost have to drag myself to work; every day and every moment are miserable. I feel a huge mismatch between the person I am and the person this job requires me to be. I feel trapped. Each day makes things seem worse. I dread the prospect of Monday morning. I take all my sick leave because the job often makes me feel ill.

Consider your results from Exercise 3.1. If you're in the first category, congratulations. Recognise what's good about your work and ensure that it remains that way. Generally, only a minority of people place themselves in the top two groups. Surveys often suggest that at least 50% of people are unhappy in their work. That's a lot of people, and a lot of days, weeks, and years wasted. US writer Studs Terkel (1974) famously recorded that work, for some, was 'a Monday to Friday sort of dying'.

If you're in the 'clock watcher' box, make a review of how you can change things – soon! As this chapter discusses, you don't need to aim for a dream job to make significant changes in your working life.

Is work that important?

Judging by the amount of time spent complaining about work, it must be. If it wasn't for work, we would have far less to moan about. We put a huge amount of energy into work, and rely on it for a large chunk of self-esteem. For this reason alone, unemployment and underemployment are damaging. Equally, people who are in work but don't feel engaged often feel that life lacks something important. As this chapter outlines, you'll spend a great deal of time in work. Work will consume a large amount of your energy, creativity, and stamina. Therefore, one thing should be clear. Choosing the work you do is one of the most important life decisions you will ever make.

Some say that they *work to live* and are only interested in how they spend the money they earn – on activities largely outside work. For some, that's entirely true. They can cope with a boring job if it funds their chosen lifestyle. As a long-term strategy that may not work – organisations know which staff are fully motivated and who is on auto-pilot, and the time may come when work is just *too* unstimulating.

Others feel that they *live to work*. For them work provides excitement, variety, friendship, or challenge. Even so, it can be important to ask if your work plays too big a part in your life. Redundancy seems to be hardest for those who have made their work their only focus, perhaps at the expense of family life or personal development. In the 1970s, an older joke was popularised by the comedian Lily Tomlin: *Even if you win the rat race, you're still a rat.*

What are the things at work that give you a buzz? The sort of things you go home and talk about? Write them down – they're worth recording, along with the things that stimulate rather less. Write down:

1. The really good stuff (things you find stimulating and enjoyable).
2. Things you could live without (that which you find boring or dull).

3. Things you put up with at work that you need like a hole in the head (the aspects of work that fill you with dread or loathing).

Good work

The Taylor Report (2017) followed an independent review for the UK Prime Minister's office considering work in the modern economy. The report calls for policy to create quality work for all, arguing that 'All work in the UK economy should be fair and decent with realistic scope for development and fulfilment'. The report adds that the pace of change in the economy, particularly in technology, means 'we need a concerted approach to work which is both up to date and responsive and based on enduring principles of fairness'.

The idea of *good work* isn't new. Economists have known for centuries that certain kinds of work are intrinsically fulfilling, and other kinds of work are draining and have a negative effect on workers. There are many modern indicators of what 'good' work looks like, and they all tend to include not just the safety, health, and well-being of workers but other factors such as job security, workers' rights, and fair wages. Definitions often also include reference to lifelong learning and career development, diversity, and work–life balance. What good work looks like as we spend more time working at a distance from colleagues remains to be seen.

Work impacts on a wide range of people. You may have family who rely on the income you provide, but they may also bear the cost of your commitment to work. Matthew Fox (1994) wrote, 'Behind some parental compulsion to bring home exaggerated amounts of pay is often a flight from the joy of living life here and now in the family – as if the future were more important than the present ... We ought not to postpone living because of work or because of our plans for buying something with the money we make'.

What you get out of work, and what work gets out of you

My grandfather Owen Roberts had a way with words in both Welsh and English. For example, he said *I eat well, I sleep well, and when I think about work I tremble all over.* It wasn't true, of course. He spent many happy years working as a dockside blacksmith.

Although we sometimes enjoy complaining about work, evidence suggests that in the past 30 years work satisfaction has declined. One reason most commonly cited is lengthening working hours. The charity Working Families (2019) recorded that 44% of UK working parents said they dip into work (for example, checking emails) when they get home. For 73% this wasn't a positive choice but a requirement – either to keep on top of their job, or to keep their manager happy. Many in the survey talked about the way technology often means that work expands into family time. The Mental Health Foundation (2020) found that, 'The cumulative effect of increased working hours is having an important effect on the lifestyle of a huge number of people, which is likely to prove damaging to their mental well-being'.

A CIPD Survey (2019) measuring the impact of work on family life places the UK 24th out of 25 economies in terms of quality of work–life balance. The survey indicates that 'Overwork is most common among managerial and professional workers. It is also more common among those who work from home, showing that flexible working may not always solve tensions between work and personal life and may even contribute to the blurring of the boundaries between them'. A YouGov report (2017) recorded that having an unhelpful work–life balance makes employees feel disengaged and left feeling 'alienated by modern life'.

There are other factors too: people seem to have high expectations of career variety and satisfaction, and an idealised view of the way employers might look after their long-term interests. Many of us are fazed by downsizing, failing organisations, and job uncertainty. While some are in danger of burnout, others have too little work. For some, working in isolation or 'hot-desking' removes the social element from work.

You need a strategy to help you find a job that builds you up more than it breaks you down.

The days of your life

If you think you can get by with a so-so job, you might be ignoring the huge amount of time that work consumes. We like to think we have the power to make life choices, but for most people work is the dominating life event. If you work full-time hours, you spend more time in work than in any other waking activity (if you live for 70 years, you'll spend about 23 of those years asleep and 16 years working). Work consumes a great deal of your best stamina and concentration. You will spend at least 100,000 hours in work. That's 'in work' – what Americans call 'face time', the time when your jacket is on the back of your chair. Work cultures have shifted fast since we first became interested in work–life balance. Organisations now expect work to be done out of hours. Also, think about the additional hours you put into worrying about work, or complaining about work.

According to UK government statistics, females born in this decade can expect an average lifespan of just under 83 years. Call it 32,000 days. Men get rather less – about 29,000 days. So, maybe 30,000 days to learn, work, play, raise a family, leave your mark on life, and acquire wisdom. If you get to the age of 50, on average you'll get longer than this, but even so, 30,000 days doesn't sound like a lot of time, does it? Especially if you're saying, 'this isn't what I wanted to do when I grew up . . .'.

Why should people be happy at work?

It's easy to believe that work is not somewhere you're supposed to enjoy yourself. We create a world of compartments: this is the compartment where I work; this is my family compartment; this small compartment is where I am myself. It's all part of that either/or thinking we're so good at (see Chapter 4 for the games we play with 'ideal' and 'real').

There is a kind of strange career pact we seem to make keeping us in either/or mode. This pact assumes 'I can only be successful if . . .'. Here are some examples: 'I can only be a top salesperson if I work long hours and eat badly'; 'I can only be a great manager if I don't empathise with my staff'. Listen to the language people use when they decide to compromise. They 'settle for' choices they're not really comfortable with. They 'lower their sights'. They pretend they are being logical and sensible.

Why should people be happy at work? Work isn't fun, your friends will tell you. Work is about hard-nosed reality. If that sounds like a universal truth, look again at the people who seem to get the most out of their jobs. They're often making new things happen, sharing what they know, sometimes inspiring people. Some are in jobs that directly improve the lives of others. Others are producing brilliant ideas, products, or great experiences for customers. Are these workers richer or poorer as a result? Happiness and success don't always come hand in hand, but being unhappy is no automatic route to success. Unfortunately, it's often the unhappy, unenthusiastic, low-energy people that companies get rid of first. Some workers are successful and paid well simply because they have found work that channels their best energy.

Why should people be happy at work? Take a deep breath. Read that question again. Work is where you spend most of your waking life. It's where you put about 80% of your best energy. Yes, you have energy for things outside your job, but for most of us working in what is increasingly becoming a 24/7 economy, most of our stamina, imagination, and personal energy will be expended on work. Work matters. It may be one of the things in life that contributes most to self-esteem and a sense of fulfilment. In today's world, choosing how you spend Monday to Friday is probably one of the most important life decisions you make.

So the question *why should people be happy at work?* really means *why should people be happy?* What do you think? Do happy people live longer, stay healthier, have great children, and make a difference? You know they do. So let's stop that Faustian deal: 'I can only get a great job if I forget about being happy at work'. That's a self-fulfilling deal. Be careful what you ask for – you might just get it.

Happiness – goal or accident?

Are some occupations more satisfying than others? We seem to have a fascination with the worst jobs in society, and a hunger to find jobs which offer the greatest job satisfaction. Popularity contests are sometimes won by surprising job roles (statisticians and web designers), and perhaps more predictably by roles with tangibly positive outcomes, for example childcare workers, fitness coaches, and bar workers. Low job satisfaction is often recorded among teachers, social workers, and health sector workers.

It's worth saying a little more about happiness. Many of us think that happiness is a vague, subjective, and entirely individual state of mind. Others believe that we can do very little to influence or adjust happiness. Richard Layard (2005) shows that happiness can be measured objectively, and explores why some nations are happier than others. Layard finds that being happy contributes to good health. He also argues that being rich doesn't make people happier (although not having enough to live on certainly reduces happiness). Many countries in the developing world with low income levels per capita are just as content as developed nations, and in some cases happier. Additionally, there is little to suggest that achieving ever greater income levels measurably increases contentment.

This has consequences for career planning. Think about factors which contribute to *your* long-term happiness, including mental and physical health, family relationships, friendships, or belonging to a community. Many people find that happiness comes from helping others. Work plays a big part – being unemployed or underemployed damages self-esteem, and meaningful work builds it.

Layard also found that what makes workers unhappy or ill isn't generally working hard or putting in long hours – contented workers often have some control over *how* they work. If you can predict your workload and make decisions about how you tackle your Inbox, that can help.

Getting more excited about the 9 to 5

Career specialists talk about *motivated skills* – the skills you relish using. There's a big difference between doing something because you know how, and doing it because it feels worth doing. That difference is the power of motivation. Motivation turns an errand into a quest, a task into a joy.

Career exploration depends on the motivation you apply to the process. *You get out what you put in.* Read that last sentence again. Your success in gaining a stunning career depends as much on your own personal motivation as it does on any other combination of factors, internal or external. And that's not all. Some of the satisfaction you will get from career exploration and success will be about meeting other people, finding out about them, making connections, and – occasionally – helping others out. So here's an important reminder in a rather self-focused age: one of the strongest factors affecting happiness is the opportunity to help other people.

Exercise 3.2 – Your Jigsaw Job

This exercise allows you to see the component parts of your ideal job without getting locked into a job title.

Imagine that you buy a jigsaw puzzle from a charity shop. The puzzle is in a plastic bag with no box, picture, or title. You don't know if the picture shows a cottage, a seascape, or a kitten. You probably begin with the edges, letting go of the question 'What does this picture show?'

Start with a feeling. Imagine you're in a fulfilling job. Don't worry what the job is called or what it says on your business card. You enjoy the role. When you're planning for work on a Sunday afternoon, you anticipate the working week positively. You've been in the role for at least 12 months and it's still stimulating. The first question is around location and setting. Imagining yourself in this 'virtual' role, what do you see around you?

Look at the example below to build up your own jigsaw job. What are your answers to the topics in the left-hand column?

Topic	Example response
Location, setting	Urban. Aesthetically pleasing building in multicultural centre. Good light. The role involves travel and meeting people
Hours	The opportunity to work from home about once a week
People	A role where I have a mentor. Trusting, cooperative environment. To be part of an enthusiastic, smart team – sharing ideas, thinking collectively

The way I manage other people	More a mentor than a supervisor. I like people I can rely on to do the job without being chased
The way I am managed	My boss is direct, honest, sees my potential. Keeps me on the straight and narrow but gives me freedom to perform tasks in my own way
Skills I use	Being the face of the organisation. Liaising, explaining; translating complex ideas into straightforward terms. Communicating/influencing. Using creative and analytical thinking
Problems	Trying to help people with their problems. Completing work on time
Challenges	Competition: something to drive me. The job is testing/stretching. Learning about managing/leadership
Values expressed	Strong ethos. Clear sense of purpose/ meaning
Likely/attractive outcomes include	Getting a team result. Bringing the best out of people. Delighting the client
General details	A firm that's large enough to help me grow, small enough to support people
The job will be rewarding because . . .	I will be achieving something. It will be fun
How work contributes to life outside work	Comfortable lifestyle. Health. Well-being
Work will allow time and energy for me to do these things outside work	Spending time with family and friends. Enjoying the theatre and cultural events again

'Must do' list

✓ Reflect on how big a part work plays in your life, and how much it contributes to your general sense of well-being.

✓ Identify someone you know who has very clearly taken control of their career. Find out their first steps, how they made change happen, and how they sustain their energy.

✓ Examine your work–life balance. How much of your energy does work require? How much energy is left for other things you'd like to do with your time?

✓ Consider: what combination of pieces in your jigsaw job would improve your long-term job satisfaction?

First steps towards a new career deal

'I like work: it fascinates me.
I can sit and look at it for hours'.
Jerome K. Jerome

This chapter helps you to:

- Look at the mix of accident, luck, and design in your career
- Understand that a new career direction will probably require new kinds of thinking
- Learn how to work smarter rather than harder at shaping your career
- Imagine possibilities for change.

Real and ideal

Career management sounds complicated, but it's really about starting a process. You begin by looking at yourself, discovering the work you will find most stimulating. You might think about your goals – financial, learning, or personal. You'll consider life–work balance – making room for learning, family, relationships, and other activities that matter.

Having looked at yourself, you look at your environment. Career management doesn't always mean job hunting. Sometimes you might want to learn something new, or renegotiate your current role so you do more of the things that energise you. However, the process can never be entirely focused on you. A career connects you to the world around you. You will look at opportunities out there in the market, some of them job-shaped. This process involves discovering work sectors (including jobs you didn't know existed) where you can make a difference. And, as you look, you might start to imagine what you might do next.

Exercise 4.1 – If all jobs paid the same ...

Ask yourself the following question: 'If all jobs paid the same, what would I do for a living?'

Mull over that question for a while, then fill in the four clouds below. You don't have to complete them in order.

In an ideal world I'd like to...

What I would enjoy about it...

Qualities I would bring to this role

Skills I would LOVE to use or learn...

Reflect on your answers to Exercise 4.1. How did you feel when you were faced with the first empty cloud? What was easy? What was difficult? For career coaches this exercise provides a great deal of information about confidence, optimism, imagination – but also about what gets in the way – the constraints and 'yes, buts' that act like lead weights on a soul hungry for flight.

I often use this exercise with groups of people because it quickly reveals the prevailing mindset in the room. Some people will be energised by what they write, while others find it difficult to commit their thoughts to paper. A small minority tell me the exercise is disconnected from the 'real world'. And that's partly what this exercise is about, to reveal where each person sits on the Ideal vs. Real spectrum. Think of it as a see-saw:

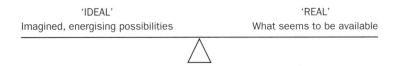

| 'IDEAL' | 'REAL' |
| Imagined, energising possibilities | What seems to be available |

Where do you sit on the see-saw most of the time? In a typical job search, people start out optimistic, believing in opportunity (see the Confidence Window, p. 150). It takes only a few rejections to push them towards the right-hand side. This can easily be accentuated when others push job advertisements under your nose, recommending that you apply for things you know you will find dull. However optimistic we feel, there is a great deal of weight on the 'real' end of the see-saw. You're thinking of doing something exciting, but people tell you to be 'realistic'.

Being 'realistic'

Listen to everyday career conversations going on around you in coffee shops. Someone asks the question, 'what are you looking for?' and the answer often begins, 'Well, in an ideal world . . .'. This first thought is often spoken with excitement. Soon the mood and body language tell a different story. The other half of the sentence is more downbeat: 'but, to be realistic . . .'. First, you talk about an interesting 'ideal' world where work might be fun. Then your focus shifts to a rather less exciting compromise – something that feels like trading down. Whether voiced or not, one word hangs over the conversation: *realistic* – the most dangerous word in the career-changer's vocabulary.

Under pressure, we like to make choices simple. We fall back on either/or thinking – trying to make choices easier by turning a multicoloured world into black and white. So, as with the overheard coffee shop career discussion, you might find yourself using one of the nation's favourite polarised statements: *I either find a job I enjoy doing, or (to be more realistic), I find a job that pays the bills.* That sentence sounds like an internal debate, but it isn't. The decision has already been made. You're going to be 'realistic'.

Let's be clear, there are problems at both ends of the see-saw. If you stay entirely in the Ideal zone, you're probably aiming at the kind of role that only comes up once in every thousand vacancies, or pushing on doors that are likely to stay closed. Advice which says 'just dream the dream' or 'you can be anything you want to be' doesn't cut it, even in a buoyant market. Are you looking at a likely career path (something you can and will do something about), or a comforting daydream?

On the other hand, a sprinkling of idealism gives you the energy you need to ask questions and seek out interesting people. The 'ideal' end of the spectrum gives you motivation to find things out. It's hard to generate enthusiasm for opportunities which are simply 'realistic', ordinary, vanilla. If you follow advice and stay 'realistic', how motivated will you be to keep on looking when things don't go so well? If you're applying for an uninspiring job, how lively will you be at interview?

Consider the Ideal/Real see-saw with a number score beneath it:

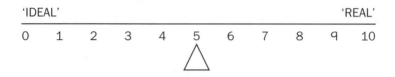

What does your score say about your thinking? If you want to feel motivated by the task, keep somewhere to the left of the mid-point. A score of around 4 balances enthusiasm with pragmatism. This means you're looking at career ideas that provoke curiosity, meeting people you find interesting. You look forward to the next conversation, and you have questions you want to ask. You get a sense that the work on offer is a fairly good match to who you are. Forget the bad press that 'ideal' receives, and all those people who tell you not to waste time looking for your dream role. You're looking for a *good deal* rather than a *perfect match.*

So-called 'realistic' thinking can stop you at the first hurdle, especially if applied too early in the process. The word *realistic* is dangerous – because it is rarely about what is real. It's usually second-hand information – someone else's picture of the world. Don't fall for the idea that 'realistic' means objective, well informed, based on reality. Whose reality? Listen to the people who are telling you to 'lower your sights'. What does that say about their own life experience and ambitions? As Chapter 2 outlined, it really pays to spend time with positive-minded people. Optimism equals energy, and energy matters if you want to change career – you'll need it to sustain you, and you'll need to communicate it to potential employers.

Seeing data, not noise

The above does *not* mean that your next move should be made without any reference to the real world of employers and hiring decisions. A proper reality check means finding out what's out there, and how you match your evidence so you get shortlisted. It's equally important to be objective about lack of progress. One rejection letter is a random event. Collect information, not hunches. If half a dozen seasoned recruitment consultants tell you there are absolute barriers to getting shortlisted, or you discover from several contacts that a sector is in terminal decline, or that your CV as it stands will prevent you getting shortlisted, that's useful, hard data. Everything else is just random noise.

This book asks you to think about dream jobs in order to see what attracts you to real jobs. Instead of looking for perfection, look for a role offering a healthy mix of the things that keep you motivated. 'Compromise' doesn't mean defeat – it can mean a healthy working understanding:

All work is a deal

between what you want out of life

and what an employer

wants out of you.

It's useful to start to think about career choice as a deal, because that means you can let go of the idea of the perfect job, and start to think about *healthy* compromise.

Aim for 70%

Once you know what you're looking for, try to resist offers
that really don't match (read about the high/low game
in Chapter 12). Aim for a good overlap, and let go of the
idea of the perfect job. Believing that only 100% will do
is in fact a great excuse to stop looking. Understand that
work is all about making deals, and *good enough* can work
for you.

Look at yourself until you're pretty sure about the kind of
role that suits you best, and the skills you'd like to use. Many
chapters in this book will help you with this, and you can
summarise your findings on one page in the **Master Sheet**
(see p. 261).

Next, look at jobs that might be available to you. Compare what you want with the employer's hit list. This means
going way beyond job descriptions – dig deep to find out
what the organisation needs and wants. When you know
this clearly (it will usually involve at least one conversation
with someone who knows the organisation well), look for
overlap between you and the job:

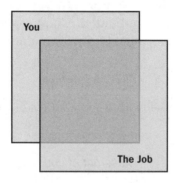

If you identify a genuine overlap of around 70%, the job
is probably a good match – you'll be happy in work about

3½ days out of 5, which is plenty. If it feels more like 50% or 60%, the role may be an acceptable stepping stone. If the match is 50% or less, watch out.

Working smarter rather than harder at career-building

Some say the perfect job is out there looking for you. However, you can't sit at home and wait for it to drag you out of bed. The majority of us have to rely on a mix of active investigation, supportive contacts, and luck. Luck has been described as two mathematical laws working together: chance and averaging. We can't control chance, but we can increase the odds in our favour. Invest in your future. Use thinking time carefully, and learn to think openly, because a moment's inspiration can sometimes take you much further than a year's dull planning.

Setting objectives is a vital part of the process. Ideas without activity are just ideas. You don't need to wait for a brilliant career idea, a lucky breakthrough, or great contacts (although any of the last three will shorten the process). What you do need is to plan to take one step, soon, and then take the step after that. That's how change happens.

Information is neutral. It's easy to put all your attention on things you believe you lack. For example, 'I can't . . .', 'I've never been good at . . .', and so on. You may discover you are really good at hanging on to these ideas, and stating them as absolute facts. Exploring is an opening-out process. We tend to think along tramlines, moving logically from one stage to the next. Divergent thinking works rather differently. Let your imagination fan out: rather than making decisions too soon, look at possibilities.

Exercise 4.2 – Career Transition Diamonds

Focusing on target
organisations and shortlists

Diamond 2

Reaching out to a range of contacts –
exploration combined with
multi-channel
job searching

Through
conversations and
research, narrowing down
ideas to focus on particular
sectors, organisations, and roles

Diamond 1

Discovering what you have to offer,
building confidence in your
message, exploring and
road-testing
career ideas

Active while thinking

Look at the **Career Transition Diamonds** above. Where are you in this process? **Diamond 1** represents the first phase of career transition. It would be easy to think that this stage is just reflective. Yes, this stage is about experimentation *and* idea-building, not just reflection. Turning ideas around in your head is far less effective than testing them out in real contexts. Experiments need a laboratory, and your best laboratory bench is the world of conversations. So even the bottom part of the lower diamond involves action – reaching out to other people to find things out, or try things out.

Open-minded experimentation during this first phase requires a promise. Promise yourself not to find early reasons to say 'no' to ideas. Gathering information means you can start closing things down, crossing the dotted line into the upper half of Diamond 1. Decide on a small number of sectors to investigate (see Chapter 10 to help you choose).

Notice that **Diamond 1** has a thicker dotted line across the centre. This represents a danger point where you may get stuck. Learning about ourselves can be fascinating and affirming, and sometimes we want to hear more. Watch for this invisible barrier to transition. If you find yourself looking for more career exercises and tests, enjoying the inner journey but reluctant to pick up the phone even to the friendliest contact, you've probably hit this barrier.

The antidote is to remember that each step should involve *doing* something – an activity focused on what's out there. As Richard Alderson points out in his 'Shift Projects' idea below, it's vitally important from day one to act as well as reflect, and to keep this balance at each stage in the process. Keep learning more about your strengths and preferences, but reach out to find out how they connect to *where work happens*. So, right now might be the moment to pick up the phone and arrange your first information interview (see Chapter 14).

Diamond 1, the investigation stage, requires you to step outside your comfort zone to discover things. **Diamond 2** moves you decisively into new kinds of action – approaching organisations, following leads, influencing decision-makers, moving towards job offers. Diamond 2 is action-focused, but still requires you to think imaginatively about how you can find new people to help you open doors. To get to **Diamond 2**, you need to make some hard decisions. What sectors? What organisations are you going to focus on? Now everything you do has a simple benchmark – *does what I am doing get me closer to a job offer?*

Testing ideas

Finding out, and following your enthusiasm, costs very little. Deciding to look is a small decision. You don't need to have a perfect target job to start the process of discovery, just a sense of curiosity. And here's a big clue: your breakthrough probably has a 5% likelihood of happening as a result of reading or thinking, and a 95% likelihood of occurring as a result of a person. Someone you already know, possibly. Or, even more likely, someone you meet in the next three months as a result of your active enquiries. So what's the first step? A conversation. Start with people you know, even if they seem very disconnected from the world you want to enter. Find opportunities to talk to people who love what they do for a living. Experiment with REVEAL interviews (see Chapter 14).

Try on ideas through practical experiment – not changing career overnight, but testing an idea, trying it on for size. These test-out events are what Richard Alderson calls 'Shift Projects'.

Shift Projects

When I was desperately unhappy in my job, I did what I thought were the sensible things to do: I spoke to recruiters, I read career books, I did psychometric tests, I made lists, and I did a lot of analysis.

Some of this helped, but none of it led me to a definitive answer as to what else I could do. Instead, I felt like I was going round and round in circles. It was only when I started to take actions in the outside world – meeting new people, doing new things, and stepping into new environments – that clarity started to emerge.

Why? Because, only in hindsight did I realise that I was trapped in my own reality bubble – the people, places, and perspectives that made up my world. If the answer to my career change challenge lay in the world around me, I would have found it. Instead, I needed to break out of my bubble.

Taking real-world actions did this for me. Not only did they reveal new career options (indeed the role I shifted into was in a field I previously didn't even know existed), but they also allowed me to test these options to see which ones were viable.

This action-learning approach has become the core of the methodology that we've used at Careershifters to help more than 10,000 people on their journeys to finding more fulfilling work.

It's based around the concept of **Shift Projects**.

Shift Projects are short experiments designed to discover or test career ideas. They have three essential qualities: they're action-based experiences (talking to people or trying things out – scrolling through Google doesn't count); they're quick, so you don't waste time on things that aren't right (think a few hours to a few weeks max.); and they're carried out with a light, curious approach (because many will be dead ends).

The following are examples of Shift Projects our clients have run:

- Alex, a project manager, volunteered part-time for a tech start-up to see how it would feel compared to the large corporate environment he'd come from.

- Michelle, an administrator, went to a culinary exhibition to explore how she could potentially turn her love of food into paid work.
- Simon, an IT consultant, started a mindfulness group in his company to test whether he could potentially grow it into a business.
- Annika, a researcher, met with an entrepreneur pioneering more sustainability in the interior design industry to learn more about her work.

In the initial stages of a career change, Shift Projects reconnect you with the things that energise you, enable you to see new career possibilities, and help you get clearer about what you really want. Critically, you often need to start running them without an initial direction, which can feel counter-intuitive.

In the latter stages of a career change, Shift Projects enable you to test and validate different specific career paths – helping you get clear on what other options would be viable, before you need to take unnecessary financial risks.

You can read more about how to create your own Shift Projects here: **www.careershifters.org/shift-projects**

Richard Alderson – founder of Careershifters

Capturing energy

Where you put your energy matters – both in terms of exploring and job hunting. In the first phase, energy translates into focused attention. If your attention goes into believing little is available and you have few skills to offer, that dark picture absorbs your energy. If you feel your glass is half empty, you're giving attention to absence – closed doors, people who didn't return your call. Try something different. *Choose* to put your energy into seeing each glass as half full. That way you begin to see possibilities, perhaps even abundance – and you see it everywhere. I love the strapline used by the Australasian car hire firm Jucy: 'The glass is half full – and the other half was delicious.'

Look for organisations, sectors, products, and roles that spark your curiosity; this energy will become a hunger to find out more. You find yourself talking enthusiastically about your discoveries to friends. If the ideas and people you encounter energise you, that keeps you active and reinforces the small bursts of confidence you need to pick up the phone, make connections, to keep looking even when initial results are unpromising.

This same energy helps in job hunting. Employers buy into what they describe as drive and attitude – they prefer motivated people. So, talk enthusiastically about the work sectors you're investigating. Make people believe that enthusiasm, and they remember you and make connections for you.

Second, capture energy from your past. Look at times when work has really motivated you – great days at work. When you talk about these events, notice how you become more animated. The energy you experienced in these moments is being re-lived. When you write and talk about your past, capture the excitement you originally felt – and communicate it. Bring past excitement into the present. This process of 'bottling energy' is clear in above-average candidates. They don't just tell stories, they re-live them.

In your CV, reveal what stimulated and enlivened you. At interview open your energy bottles to ensure you're remembered (see 'Telling tales' in Chapter 16).

Recruit a support team

Critics have argued that Jane Austen portrayed two kinds of individuals in her books: people who live and *people who see themselves living*. Self-awareness makes a difference. People who make conscious decisions about their working lives are likely to be more successful and more satisfied. They have thought about the work that they want to do and are actively pursuing it. Some have moved into new roles, and others have redesigned or renegotiated the jobs that they do.

Few things are achievable without the right tools and the right people, yet all too many job seekers try to manage the work alone. Get support.

First of all, have experimental, 'what if?' conversations with as many folk as you can who can give you a different perspective (but make sure the feedback is at least objective, and preferably upbeat). Second – and do this before you finish this book – build a support team.

Find *two* people who will meet you and provide help. They don't need to be in the same situation as you, but they do need to be curious about people, jobs, and the world. One person will do, at a push, but a coach–pupil relationship often results when there are only two people. With a trio meeting together regularly, you get two perspectives on everything that's said. The conversation doesn't need to be just about you – help each other in turn. You'll often find that a trio discussion over a cup of coffee or a bottle of wine works very nicely.

Recruit the two members of your trio carefully. They should be people who can:

- Support you in the ups and downs of career transition.
- Give you honest, objective advice about your skills, and help you to see the evidence you use to back them up.
- Provide ideas for exploration and connections with other people who can help.
- Use positive thinking to help you build on your ideas.

Warning: if you hear a friend say 'yes, but, in the real world . . .' or 'it's not that simple . . .', or even 'that won't work', don't invite them to be part of this process. There are thousands of people out there who will be all too happy to pour cold water on your ideas. Career success is as much about motivation as it is about strategy. Choose people who will give you encouraging feedback and positive support.

'Must do' list

✓ Reflect on what the word 'realistic' means for you. How much of your picture of work is based on second-hand or out-of-date information? What can you do to find out more?

✓ Work out what kind of career deal works best for you. What are the 'must have' ingredients in a new job? What can you live without?

✓ When you're considering a new role, find out what the job is really like, and see how far the reality of the role overlaps with your personal wish list.

✓ Look at the Career Transition Diamonds. Where are you now? Are you stuck in reflection? Plan your next action step.

✓ Don't get too obsessed with your CV, your interview answers, your networking 'pitch'. You get better results by discovering new organisations and finding out the different career deals on offer.

5

Thinking, deciding, and getting on with it

'If you can dream – and not make dreams your master;
If you can think – and not make thoughts your aim . . .'
Rudyard Kipling

This chapter looks at the following areas:

- Exploring how you make career decisions
- Breaking out of A to Z thinking
- Letting go of the urge to decide
- Avoiding passivity and negative reinforcement
- Idea-building and moving forward towards positive solutions.

I can't decide what kind of career I want . . .

Some decisions are easier than others. If it's obvious what job should appear next on your CV, it doesn't take much thought to name it. Other decisions are much harder, especially if you have no idea what you want to do next, can't see a way out of where you are now, or know where you want to be but don't know how to get there. Changing career requires a lot of *doing*, and a fair amount of *thinking differently*. What looks like a series of tough decisions can in fact require the ability to put decision-making to one side while you explore actively.

You might be asking yourself, 'what job would I like to do next?', but the key question is *'how are you going to find out?'* People secretly believe that the answer will come along if they take a test, read a book, or just sit at home with the curtains closed and think really, really hard. This assumes that the most useful tool available to you is *A to Z thinking* – a method which plans to move from problem to solution in a logical, straight-line path. Yes, analysing, categorising, researching, and planning are all useful. However, when you need to navigate unknown territory, imagination and curiosity will give you much better results. To do something different, to reinvent yourself and make new connections in terms of ideas and people, you need to be energised. Getting a job that floats your boat means behaving and thinking more adventurously, and this new mode needs to be inspired – by conversations and discoveries.

Become an ideas factory, hungry to discover new futures. And then act on career ideas rather than just finding evidence to shoot them down. Test them out through active research and conversations. You can't think yourself out of a hole, and you can't get perfect results through desk research – interactions with other people are the best way to find out more and open doors.

Remember, you are *not* making a final decision about your career path today. You are simply deciding to start a process, following where your curiosity takes you. Every time you find an idea that really gets your attention, take that motivation seriously: look again, and look deeply. This energy is useful; it persuades you to dig deeper, and find out more. It gives you the extra ounce of confidence you need to pick up the phone and dial. Energy has one other great quality, too – people remember you.

Marilyn Ferguson (1987) reminds us that change comes from within: 'No one can persuade another to change. Each of us guards a gate of change that can only be opened from the inside. We cannot open the gate of another, either by argument or by emotional appeal'. Push your brain into a new gear. Look at different styles of decision-making. First, be honest about your feelings about change or talking about yourself to strangers. Fear can often lead us to dismiss new ideas without collecting information objectively. Avoid saying 'no' from habit; talk career ideas through with positive colleagues.

Push ideas so you see benefits as well as pitfalls. Instead of dismissing ideas as unrealistic, ask 'how could I make this work? What could come out of this?'

Ideas Factory

Here are some suggestions for building career ideas:

- Allow yourself to generate a range of ideas, without self-criticism.
- If you feel your brain is overloaded, do something entirely different – run up a hill, watch a movie, cook. Putting your brain in a new gear is often a great way of generating ideas.
- When a new idea hits you, don't dismiss it as daydreaming. Test it out.
- Write out ideas on postcards or Post-it notes. Look for connections. See what happens when you combine two or three ideas. Prioritise your ideas so you know what to give maximum focus.
- Look for new sub-sectors (see Exercise 10.1 – Sector match, p. 129).
- Turn your sector idea upside down. For example, you may be interested in child development because you are interested in the way young people grow. Turning that upside down might lead you to thinking about the effects of ageing.
- *Do* something with every career idea – turn it into a piece of research or a conversation.

Be more experimental

Enjoy this key stage of exploration and discovery. Put your decision-hungry brain on hold. You don't have to make the one big decision about your life just yet. You need to make a choice, though – to keep looking, and to keep asking questions. Think of this process as spinning half a dozen plates in the air, giving each plate just a little extra spin every day. Exploration shouldn't be an excuse for hiding away and getting lost in Google. Involve other people in the process.

Don't be put off if you don't get amazing results overnight. Most experiments don't lead to instant success, and every new invention builds on a history of failed attempts. Resist pressure from friends, family, and professional contacts to do the next obvious thing (see Exercise 1.1 – Breaking out of default mode, p. 12). The most important work you put into your career isn't about CV writing or interview preparation, it's about *learning to think differently*.

Since a great deal of this is about imagination, you might be hiding behind the statement 'I'm not a creative person'. Let's establish a ground rule. We're all creative in some way. We are all capable of inventing creative solutions to life's varied problems, such as taking children in opposite directions in one car, paying this week's bills with next week's money, caring for three or four difficult children at their most unpleasant, or making dinner out of six things in the cupboard. We are all capable of flexible, creative thinking. We have to be: that's how humans have survived. Look for the next door to open, the next conversation to move you forward.

Shift your language

Try a change of vocabulary. Practise a register shift, from no to **yes.**

The language of NO	The language of YES
It'll never work	Let's look at our alternatives
It's how I am; I was born that way	I can try a different approach
She makes me behave like that	I control my own feelings

It's against the rules	I'll invent a new rulebook
It's not for me	I need to find out more
I'm forced to	I will choose
In the real world . . .	I make my world real by . . .
Another mistake . . .	How interesting . . .
If only . . .	Let's try . . .
Never	It's all experimental

Distinguish between goals and dreams

Most of us like daydreams where work is easy and pays well. Maybe you dream about running a small and highly profitable bar on a beach somewhere, where the weather is glorious and the hours are short. These dreams are fun, something to keep us warm on cold winter nights, and they are also entirely *safe* – you never have to do anything about them. Daydreams are a form of fantasy entertainment. A goal is very different – you need to do something about it.

Some people believe that success arrives by creating big, adventurous goals and sticking to them with fanatical commitment. In his book *59 Seconds* (2010), Richard Wiseman debunks some of these goal-setting myths, such as the unfounded idea that if you write down your life-changing goals they are more likely to happen. There is no research data to support this idea. However, there is evidence to suggest that short-term goal-setting is highly effective. If you break tasks down into mini-objectives and reward yourself for achieving them, you're more likely to make progress. Real goals require a first, second, and third step.

This can sound a little over-processed. Don't lose sight of the original fascination you experienced when you came across an idea for exploration. If something draws you, it gives you the energy to step outside your comfort zone and make something happen. Ideas should lead to actions.

Sometimes this means active experiment (see the first steps in Chapter 4), and 99% of the time you need to find someone to talk to.

Reinventing your career self

Can people reinvent themselves? Some of us have no choice. In a rapidly changing world, we may need to do this more than once. Reshaping your career requires you to remain open to possibilities, forever curious and willing to try on new ideas. Learn how to cultivate tentative plans for exploration rather than trash them. It's no use thinking 'I wonder about medicine . . .' if you immediately say 'Do I want to be a doctor or don't I?' Forcing a decision too early simply crushes creative thinking. Maybe not a doctor – maybe a medical journalist, a pharmacist, a nutritionist, or a physiotherapist?

If reinvention is on your radar, think about how you have made decisions in your career so far – the paths you have followed, and paths not taken.

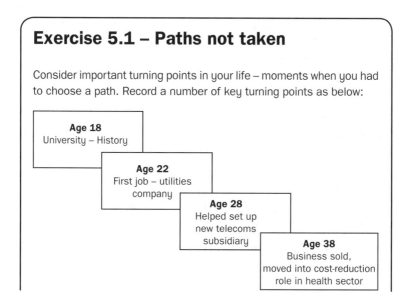

Exercise 5.1 – Paths not taken

Consider important turning points in your life – moments when you had to choose a path. Record a number of key turning points as below:

Age 18
University – History

Age 22
First job – utilities company

Age 28
Helped set up new telecoms subsidiary

Age 38
Business sold, moved into cost-reduction role in health sector

Look at **one** of your turning points. Write it in a box in the middle of a piece of paper. Then draw out your **paths not taken as below**.

These are the alternative choices which were on offer at the time – things you nearly did or could have done. Your final diagram might look like the following example:

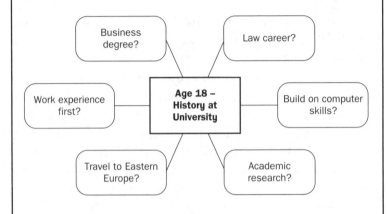

Questions about your paths not taken:

- What choices were available to you at past turning points?
- How did you choose each path?
- What difference would a change of path have made to you?
- How have you made career decisions since?

Make it so

Do it as if all jobs pay the same. Do it as if all doors will open for you. Do it as if you were doing it for somebody else. Imagine a friend offers you a thousand pounds to find *her* ideal career path. If you took the task on, you wouldn't go back every 5 minutes saying 'you wouldn't like this', yet this is what we do for ourselves. If you were doing it for someone else, you'd keep looking for variations and angles, keep turning up new connections. Start by simply generating ideas for roles and sectors worth investigating.

Look for things that tickle your curiosity, areas you find you talk about with enthusiasm – these are big clues to your future.

In various incarnations of *Star Trek*, Captain Jean-Luc Picard (played by the inimitable Patrick Stewart) executed commands with three plain words: *Make it so*. There comes a point when it's healthy to move on from 'what if' to 'how could I make this work?' Think in terms of pilot schemes and experiments – low-risk ways of getting things moving. Extend yourself by studying in your own time. Take up voluntary activity outside work in order to experiment with your career longings. Short-term or temporary employment can sometimes help to provide a useful 'laboratory' for your career plans. Sometimes the best prompt for everyday experiment is: 'Don't think, just leap'.

Ruts and channels

One of the reasons people accept uninspiring work is that human beings are adaptable. We can live in climates ranging from Arctic cold to sweltering heat. We can survive in the most unhealthy and difficult conditions, and families can work, raise children, and live good lives even under the most brutal political regimes. Perhaps because of this built-in survival instinct, some of us have the capacity to do something that modern society finds odd and most of history saw as the norm. We can hold down an uninspiring job for decades. Given a world of choice, the fact that we can doesn't mean that we should.

People often say they are stuck in a career rut. The worst kind of rut is the *velvet rut*: you hate being in it, but it's just too comfortable to climb out of. Ruts stay ruts because you're stuck in your thinking. You know that something needs to change, but what? What's needed is breakthrough thinking, a great idea to move you forward. What you're probably going to need is to think a little differently, and behave a little differently.

Define the problem you'd like to solve in terms of a future emotional state. How would you like to feel in a year's time? What changes in you would others notice? What first step can you take tomorrow to make that change a possibility?

The fashion designer Ozwald Boateng was interviewed on BBC Radio 4's Midweek programme in March 2012. He mentioned that his father's career advice was that if something 'came easy' to Ozwald, he should stick at it. So he did, switching from a course in computer studies to fashion. His father quickly said that this wasn't what he had in mind, but Boateng stuck at it and has built a highly successful business with an international reputation. Your talents are not always evident until you discover them, but if you find something you do well that 'comes easy', it's a great place to start.

Many years ago I heard a motivational speaker in San Francisco deliver a great one-liner. I've tried to find the speaker's name, without success, but I thank him anyway. He said: *If you only live half your life, the other half will haunt you forever.*

Behaviour and belief

The greatest barriers between you and an inspired career are not in the marketplace or on your CV, but in your mind. Rule 1: we know that **behaviour follows belief**. If you believe evidence of your own ability, you are more likely to talk about your strengths credibly. If you feel confident and in control, that's how you'll act. So, believe in what you can do. Learn to accept your brain's own ability to create ideas, possibilities, connections, and to put thinking into practice.

It's often said that the creative mind can hold contradictory ideas at the same time. So to Rule 2: **belief follows**

behaviour. In other words, acting out a part makes us think differently, and *it's easier to act your way into a new way of thinking than to think your way into a new way of acting.*

Try it. Behave as if you are already successful. Richard Rohr (1999) wrote: 'We do not think ourselves into new ways of living, we live ourselves into new ways of thinking'. For example, as you prepare to give a talk in public, decide now that on arrival you will act walk, and talk as if you already have the full attention of your audience. Sit down for a job interview as if you're already working successfully in the role. Walk the walk, talk the talk, and something happens – you physically act your way into a new way of looking at yourself. That's why it's easier to have authority if you are dressed professionally, and why people are more assertive on the phone when they stand up. If you act confident or proficient, you become it – quicker than you imagine.

Stop looking for negative reinforcement

There are more varieties of jobs out there than ever before, yet we still generally let our careers be shaped by accident, or accept second-best because it's easier to stand still than to move forward. Most importantly of all, we insist on using the most limited kind of straight-line thinking in career planning and job search. Why? Essentially, we like to do what feels safe, even if that means being unhappy. There's a powerful part of the brain that says: *Stop here. It's dull, but it's comfortable. Out there looks difficult and strange.*

And then you find evidence to support your position. You focus on stories of people of your age and background who tried to make a change and failed. I have a theory. At times when change threatens, we develop a personal radar that scans the horizon for information. Radar, as you know, is hungry for enemy objects. And we find them. You suddenly discover people who were made redundant and never found a job again. People beat a path to your door to tell you, *Don't do it . . . it will all end in tears.*

We come up with all kinds of negative messages to act as blocks to growth and change. If you believe you're 'not an ideas-person' or 'not a leader', your brain is capable of making sure this becomes a self-fulfilling prophecy. If a golfer says, 'I bet I slice this ball', she probably will.

I'm indebted to Marie Brett, who told a story at one of my masterclasses for career coaches. She overheard two women on a bus in Northumberland talking about one of their daughters. 'These days', one explained, 'it's not about what you *want* to do, it's about what you *can* do'. Marie could hear the poor daughter's career derailed in one sentence. Another coach, Esi Kpeglo, talked about trying to reposition herself mid-life, building on her professional background. An elderly relative suggested, with real kindness, that it might be time to find a 'humbler' job like being a pot washer or postal worker. Other people shape our career thinking, and can easily reinforce a negative picture of the world.

Focus on what's working, not on what isn't

Trainee airline pilots are taught a special thought process for emergencies. If an engine fails, they are trained not to put their entire focus onto that one component. Instead, they ask: 'What do I have left working which will get my passengers safely on the ground?' In the same way, we need to learn to shift our attention away from the things that are not working, and consciously place it on the things that are. What working strategies are still working for you? Otherwise, it's easy to expend energy on conversations that haven't worked, applications that fell at the first hurdle, or people who won't return your call. Everyone gets knock-backs. If you are the kind of person who takes rejection personally, don't beat yourself up about it – recruit some support.

Exercise 5.2 – Work themes

Starting from the inside means putting together a recipe for the kind of job that will work for you. One simple index of whether the job will work well for you is to think about the big themes that characterise work.

Scoring: Give each work theme a score between 1 and 5, where 1 = little interest, 3 = moderate interest, 5 = high interest.

Creativity Score:	Your preferred work is mainly about working imaginatively with ideas or designs; for example, the arts, performing, creative writing, visual design, lateral thinking, business creativity, adapting ideas, coming up with new ideas, challenging assumptions.

Hands On Score:	Your preference is working hands on, engaging with the physical world; for example, building, shaping, cooking, craft, DIY, working with animals, plants, machines, vehicles, sports, physical fitness, physiotherapy, or working outdoors.

Influence Score:	Your preference is working with and through other people and will involve: leadership, management, changing organisations, setting up a new business or department, inventing, reorganising, shaping teams, driving others, influencing, persuading, motivating, selling, getting results.

Information	Your ideal work is mainly about working with information; for example, analysing, cataloguing, gathering, planning, managing projects, researching, tracking down information, working with numbers or accounts, making the most of computers.
Score:	

Systems	You are most attracted to working with systems; for example, processes, quality control, continuous improvement, legal processes, procedures, bookkeeping, record-keeping, database management, health and safety.
Score:	

People	Your preference is for working with people; for example, training, teaching, coaching, mentoring, developing, caring, nursing, nurturing, healing.
Score:	

Look at your top three work themes. How is your career a unique interaction between these themes? How can you make sure that your work feeds all three? For example, if your top three work themes in order are *Creativity, People,* and *Hands On*, you'll want to ensure that your work allows you a high degree of creativity generated by teams of people, with the chance to invent new rules from time to time, but you'll be happiest working where you achieve results that you can see and feel. Remember, your work theme combination is unique to you, because it also draws upon your knowledge, values, and experience.

'Must do' list

✓ Practise using different ways of thinking and decision-making. Try a range of techniques for idea-generation (start by using them on everyday problems and then adapt them to career planning).

✓ Take dreams seriously, and see which ones will translate into goals. Write them down, somewhere, and tell someone you've done it.

✓ Write a Plan A for the next 12 months. Things to include: first steps on the journey, measurable goals, the critical steps you need to follow to make things happen (writing articles, going to conferences, talking to people, getting your CV rewritten, finishing that book . . .).

✓ Look at your top three work themes. If you combine the three together, what ideas can you come up with?

✓ Record times when you were totally absorbed in tasks – either in work or outside it. What were you doing? What kind of roles involve tasks of this kind?

✓ Where do you need to *think* more and *do* less? Be careful not to throw yourself at the job market without being prepared (see 'rookie mistakes' in Chapter 15).

✓ Where do you need to *do* more and *think* less? Where do you need to make decisions, or put decision-making aside and explore? What do you need to *do*, today?

6

What drives you?

'And nothing to look backward to with pride,
And nothing to look forward to with hope.'
Robert Frost

This chapter offers opportunities to:

- Look at workplace turn-offs
- Think about the part money plays in your career
- Identify what motivates you
- Discover your career hot buttons.

Turn-offs in the workplace

Go back to 'The good, the bad, and the just plain awful' on
p. 29. Think about your hate list: the ten things you would
like to change most (about the work you do, or the way you
are at work). You might find it helpful to categorise some of
your dissatisfactions: physical work environment, location,
colleagues you work with, management style, status, recognition, people, tasks, variety, values of the organisation,
and so on. Make sure you have recorded all the things that
demotivate or irritate you.

If you're asked why you want to leave a job, you use
shorthand: 'The job stinks', 'The money's rotten', 'My boss'.
Now look at the flip side, the positive. What parts of the
job encouraged you to head into work on a cold Monday

morning? What parts of a job keep you interested, excited, focused? Everyone has career hot buttons – the things that keep us motivated in the long term.

What really motivates you?

Recruiters will tell you that the first answer to this question is often 'money'. The reason is that it's easy, convenient shorthand. You may not be motivated by money at all, in fact. Throwing money at a problem does not make satisfied workers, and pay is rarely the *primary* motivator in changing jobs unless someone is earning way below their potential. Sometimes workers take a pay cut for the right role. For a small proportion of people, earning at a high level is like an internal game. Most people want to feel moderately well paid. Once pay issues are resolved, deeper motivators kick in – being respected for your expertise, seeing the job through to the finish, making a difference, or opportunities to keep learning.

Pain and reward

Psychologists tell us that generally we are more influenced by loss than gain. Bad news sticks longer in memory than good news. Finding £10 in the street may cheer you up briefly, but losing £5 from your pocket can taint the whole day. High pay helps to keep workers, but doesn't necessarily make them more productive. If you receive a new year pay rise, you will probably have forgotten about it within a month, but if you receive a pay cut, it will bother you every time you see your salary hit your bank account and every time you speculate about what your friends are earning. Feeling underpaid, especially where you feel your work is not appreciated, has a long-term demotivating effect.

How do you have any sense of what you are worth? I have known individuals being interviewed for £40,000 and

£80,000 jobs in the same week, with little real difference in responsibility or complexity. Markets often do very odd things with salaries. Have you ever calculated what you really cost your employer, including overheads, and then calculated what value you add to the bottom line, whether actual in terms of profits or metaphorically in terms of your invisible contribution?

When asked 'How much money do you need to feel that you have enough?', I'm told that most people name a figure which is double their present income, whether they earn £15,000 or £150,000 a year. However, most careers books ask you to work out the minimum you need to pay all your bills and to eat. Unfortunately, far too many people confuse this figure with what they are worth.

Exercise 6.1 – Earnings review

What do you need to earn each month? £ _____
i.e. when you have added up all your monthly bills, travel, insurance, health, and food costs

What do you need to live on? £ _____
i.e. what would you need to earn to be relaxed about what you spend each month?

What would be ENOUGH? £ _____
i.e. how do you value your skills, knowledge, and commitment? What do people with your skills and experience earn in your sector? If you know the earnings range, what do you have to do to be in the top 25%? Insert an annual figure here

What are you worth? £ _____

Now think ahead. Assuming you keep motivated, keep learning, and move forward in your career:

What do you want your annual earnings to be in 5 years' time?

£ _____

Some people overestimate their earning power, but this usually means they have not put enough work into matching their strengths against actual market opportunities. You know that goals are best achieved through small steps (see Chapter 5), so what are you going to do next? What can you do today to discover your market value? What first step will move you towards an interesting *and* relatively well-paid job?

Exercise 6.2 – The 3-Minute Motivation Checklist

What motivates you to get up in the morning and go to work?

You have £20 to spend on yourself. Spend it in the table below on the things that really motivate you in work. You might spend £20 on one item, or spread your money around (don't use units smaller than £1).

	Motivating factor	£££s
1	**Status** My worth is recognised in my job title/pay level/car/responsibilities . . .	
2	**Recognition** I am recognised for my skills and contribution	
3	**Feedback** I know when I am doing a good job	
4	**Skills balance** My opportunities and skills are well matched	
5	**Challenge** I like to take on new projects and problems	
6	**Leadership** I enjoy opportunities to lead others.	
7	**Personal development** I have continuing opportunities to keep learning	

8	**Variety** My work is varied and interesting	
9	**Responsibility** I am responsible for important things/people/projects	
10	**Intellectual challenge** I like to be stretched and to improve my expertise	
11	**Independence/freedom** I have some control over how I spend my time at work and where I go	
12	**Fun** I like being in lively, companionable groups that enjoy working together	
13	**Team membership** I enjoy being part of an active, supportive team	
14	**Making a difference/contributing** I can see what my contribution adds to the whole process	
15	**Helping others** My work contributes to others, or to society as a whole	
16	**Meaning and fulfilment** I find my work meaningful and fulfilling	
17	**Security** Knowing what I will be doing and earning in a year's time matters to me	
18	**Earnings now** I am relatively well paid compared with my peers	
19	**Earnings potential** My earnings will probably increase significantly in the future	
20	**Fringe benefits** The job has interesting perks	

Building on the 3-Minute Motivation Checklist

Review the motivators you have chosen. How different is this list from the way you would have completed it five or ten years ago? Motivators often change a great deal.

This exercise has been used more than any other in this book – with thousands of clients, workshop and conference delegates. Feedback reveals different ways it helps people making a career change:

1. Compare your scores with the job you're in at the moment. What drivers are missing from your current role? What difference would it make to you if more of them were present?
2. You can use it as a checklist of the ingredients you'd prefer to have in your next role (you won't get them all – see the 70% overlap on p. 48).

Look at where you have allocated £2 or more. Think about a time in work when that motivator was matched. Find someone to talk to about that experience. Make it one of the energised stories you prepare for interviews.

Exercise 6.3 – Career hot buttons

Read all the questions below and then circle the overall score you feel is right in each category. Use the full scale rather than bunch all your scores in the middle.

1. Financial rewards
• How important is the money? How energised would you be if your salary increased by 10%? 20%? How long would that feeling last?
• How motivated are you by financial rewards such as bonus payments?
• If you could do more of the interesting things in your job and fewer of the dull things, would you be just as happy with less money?
• When you're at a party and listening to people talk about their jobs, how much do you think about what they earn? How much does it matter to you if you're earning less than other people whose skills are no better than yours?

Financial rewards are:

1	2	3	4	5	6	7	8	9	10
Unimportant			Moderately important				Very important		

2. Influence

- How much do you enjoy leadership and persuasion (high influence)?
- How much control do you like to have over people, situations, problems?
- How much does it trouble you when you have little influence over decisions?
- Do you prefer to be in charge (high influence) or are you happy to follow a good leader (low influence)?
- How much do you like to have a say in change?

Influence is:

1	2	3	4	5	6	7	8	9	10
Unimportant			Moderately important				Very important		

3. Expertise

- How important is the feeling of being knowledgeable, skilled, expert?
- Are you generally happy knowing a lot about one focused area of knowledge?
- Do you enjoy a reputation as a specialist (high expertise) or are you flexible enough to take on a wide range of tasks (low expertise)?
- Do you enjoy it when others seek you out to ask for your advice or specialist knowledge?

Having expertise is:

1	2	3	4	5	6	7	8	9	10
Unimportant			Moderately important				Very important		

4. Independence

- How far do you prefer a mentor to a supervisor?
- Are you a self-starter? How much do you like to set your own deadlines?

- How much control do you like over how you will allocate your time in achieving a task?
- How important is it to you that you can decide how you spend your time?
- Do you like to have control over what you do (high independence) or are you happy to accept intelligent supervision (mid to low independence)?

Independence at work is:

1	2	3	4	5	6	7	8	9	10
Unimportant			Moderately important				Very important		

5. Relationships

- How important to you are close relationships at work?
- Do you intend to make friends through work?
- Are you more productive working in a team (high relationships) or quietly on your own (low relationships)?
- How important is it to you to trust and be trusted?

Relationships at work are:

1	2	3	4	5	6	7	8	9	10
Unimportant			Moderately important				Very important		

6. Security

- How financially secure do you need to feel?
- How much does it matter that you have a nest egg, a safety net – a cushion against ill fortune (high security)?
- How happy are you to take on risks of various kinds (low security)?
- How important is to know what you will be doing next year?

Security in work is:

1	2	3	4	5	6	7	8	9	10
Unimportant			Moderately important				Very important		

7. Status

- How much does your reputation matter to you?
- How important is it to you to have your skills recognised by your colleagues, your profession, your community (high status)?

- How far are you happy to work in the background, getting the job done, not minding who gets the credit (low status)?
- How important is it to you to have a job title that reflects the level and impact of your job?

Status is:

1	2	3	4	5	6	7	8	9	10
Unimportant			Moderately important				Very important		

8. Meaning and fulfilment

- How strongly do you feel about the value your work adds to your community or society at large?
- How aware are you of the damage your work might be doing to others, or to the environment?
- Do you hear yourself saying that your work should be *meaningful*?
- Are you happy to seek meaning outside your working life?

My search for meaning through work is:

1	2	3	4	5	6	7	8	9	10
Unimportant			Moderately important				Very important		

9. Imagination

- How much do you enjoy coming up with ideas or new ways of doing things?
- Do you prefer to let others come up with ideas while you do the detailed planning?
- Do you prefer to follow a system or set of rules (low imagination)?
- Or do you like to come up with new solutions to problems (high imagination)?

Using imagination at work is:

1	2	3	4	5	6	7	8	9	10
Unimportant			Moderately important				Very important		

Transfer your scores below:

Career hot buttons – results	
Career hot button	**Score**
1. Financial rewards	
2. Influence	
3. Expertise	
4. Independence	
5. Relationships	
6. Security	
7. Status	
8. Meaning and fulfilment	
9. Imagination	

Now list your top 4 hot buttons below, in rank order. This may bo straightforward, but you may find you have items with the same score. If so, make a decision about what matters most in a job. (For example, if your scores for **Influence** and **Status** are the same, ask yourself: 'Would I prefer a job where influence is *marginally* more important than status?')

My top 4 Career hot buttons
1.
2.
3.
4.

Building on the career hot buttons

Look at your top four buttons, and think about your present or most recent role. How many of these drivers does the role satisfy? What's missing? What can you add to your present job, or seek in your next post?

(Occupational psychologist Stuart Robertson built on these career hot buttons when designing his very interesting Career Motivation Indicator. See www.careermotivation.co.uk)

'Must do' list

- ✓ When have you felt really motivated? Think of concrete examples: projects, occasions, teams.
- ✓ What blend of job ingredients might keep you motivated in the long term?
- ✓ What do you find dull and unstimulating?
- ✓ What demotivates you in work?
- ✓ How can you identify roles which are a better match for your career drivers?

Celebrating your skills

'When love and skill work together, expect a masterpiece.'
Charles Reade

This chapter helps you to:

- Map your hidden skills – the parts of your experience you take for granted
- Understand and communicate your motivated skills
- Communicate your skill set to your colleagues, managers, and potential employers
- Express skills and achievements as mini-narratives
- Generate job ideas by combining skills.

Rediscovering your skills

You use skills every day and see others using them, so you think you're good at identifying them. In fact, many people have a limited understanding of what they do well. Colleagues may affirm your skills, but like any manager conducting an appraisal, they focus most on skills seen as valuable to the organisation. Even close friends don't see your full skill set and may not know what you enjoy doing most.

Even if you are aware of your skills, you may find it hard to talk about them. Talking about skills can feel like making hollow claims without real evidence. When an interviewer asks 'what are your top skills?', many candidates look blank.

Eventually they list skills they have used in recent roles, or talk vaguely about skills which they think will impress the interviewer.

Skills are the building blocks of work, the raw material that transforms a job description into activity that creates results. We need to be secure knowing what skills we possess, hungry to develop them, and comfortable talking about where we can make things happen.

Example: Bill uses his computer every day, but his real interest is natural history. He gives time freely to his local school, which asks him to come in to fix computer problems or advise on software. If he is invited to do anything with the children, it usually involves explaining something about computers. He's great at it: probably the best person the school can find. But what he really wants to do is to talk to the kids about pond life.

Exercise 7.1 – Skills catalogue in 10 steps

Take a pad of paper. List your skills using the ten steps below. Make sure you write down *skills* (for example, organising, planning, negotiating), not aspects of personality (for example, enthusiastic, reliable, calm).

1 Imagine it's Sunday night and you are looking forward to work tasks in the week ahead. What activities do you look forward to most?
2 Imagine you're having a brilliant day at work. If someone was following you round with a video camera, what activities would the recording show?
3 Think of the most enjoyable job you've ever done. What skills were you using?
4 Think of a project you look back on with pride. What skills were you using?

5 Think about a time when you surprised yourself by doing something you didn't know you were capable of doing. What was the skill you used?

6 Think about times when you have received praise for your work performance. What skills were mentioned?

7 What skills come easily to you – what are you naturally good at?

8 Write down any other skills you are good at *and* you enjoy using.

9 Look at all the skills you have recorded in steps 1–8. If you could choose only one skill from this list, which one energises you most?

10 Finally, think about a day at work when you were entirely absorbed in what you were doing, time passed quickly, and you went home feeling a 'buzz'. Find someone to talk to about that day, and ask them to make a list, while you are talking about all the skills you were using. Add any new skills to your list.

Exercise 7.1 gives you a useful starting list of skills you've noticed and those valued by others. If you want to cross-check this list or find better phrases to describe your skills, try the **JLA Skill Cards** (see p. 98).

Now you have a good basic list of the skills you have, you might find it helpful to see how these skills fit into different **skill categories**, for example:

- Skills connected with **information** (researching, managing data, analysing).
- Skills connected with **imagination** (creating, designing, building).
- Skills connected with **systems** (organising, planning, understanding processes and structures).
- Skills connected with **growth** and **enterprise** (making new things happen, being an entrepreneur).
- Skills connected with **influencing people** (selling, communicating, negotiating, leading, driving change).
- Skills connected with **developing people** (coaching, training, mentoring).

Unwrap your gifts

Few of us see what a well-equipped skills toolbox we've been given. We use skills without recognising or crediting them; we fail to bring our latent talents, blinking, into the light. You have been given a unique set of talents. Unique not because of one, primary, virtuoso skill that commends you to the world, but because of the way all your skills are uniquely combined in you. Unique because you are the only person with your skills, exercised through your personality, your history, your viewpoint. No one else can be you, in your particular situation in life. You can always find somebody who can employ a particular skill better than you, but they can't *be you*.

However, be careful how you think about *transferable* skills. Candidates of every generation assume that someone else makes the transfer happen. In other words, it's the employer's job to see how skills used in a previous role can be used in a new one. Skills don't transfer themselves – translate what you've done into language that an employer understands and finds attractive. If your stated skills seem to place you in a different world, you may not even get shortlisted. Some skills gain high currency overnight – for example, organising and managing online meetings.

Employers see many candidates who claim to be skilled but fail to provide supporting evidence – for example, *I am a good communicator*. What kind of communication? What do you mean by good? Say something about the level of your skills and about the context: *I regularly communicated difficult messages to team members, keeping them informed and motivated – resulting in improved staff retention over a three-year period of organisational change.*

The skills below your radar

Some of us have skills we can describe well, but there are huge areas of unmapped territory. How many of your skills fit one of the following categories?

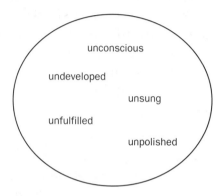

Unconscious skills

Unconscious skills are the skills you use so frequently they have become invisible to you. I call them 'wallpaper skills'. You're aware of new wallpaper for a month or so, and then gradually stop noticing it. It jumps back into focus when someone comments on your redecoration. You notice your 'wallpaper' skills when others see them. It's useful when people remind you what you're good at, especially when they see skills which you no longer notice.

Example: Maureen's great skill is untangling messy personal situations. She helps people see things clearly, encouraging parties to put anger aside and seek common ground. Others see her oiling the wheels, mending broken relationships. She was entirely unaware of this until a friend said, 'Do you know what you do? You're the cement between the bricks of our community'. She never gets the opportunity to use these skills at work, so she says nothing about them in her CV.

Example: Norma can't walk past a piece of fabric without touching it. She has a good eye for texture, colour, and pattern, and for matching materials simply and cheaply to make a room look great. She has a knack of walking into a room and knowing how to make it look more appealing in a few simple changes. Last year her friend brought out these 'wallpaper' skills and suggested she explores becoming a 'house doctor', offering low-cost design solutions to sell houses quickly.

Sometimes these are skills you use only occasionally, perhaps under pressure or in special moments. You often don't notice yourself exercising these skills in the heat of the moment, or you don't claim ownership: things just happen. In an emergency, for example, there is often someone present who has great clarity of mind, organising people, calling an ambulance and preventing panic.

Undeveloped skills

We're often very good at talking about the skills we lack, or the skills we feel are not up to scratch. You might gain more by focusing on skills that you have never really had the opportunity to develop, skills you instinctively feel you might be good at if you only had the chance.

How do you know they are there? Think about the skills you admire in others, or times when you have watched someone at work and thought, 'I wouldn't mind having a go at that . . .'. Sometimes curiosity can quickly lead to new skills. Stretch yourself. Have a go.

Example: Nick is a keen photographer but lacks confidence in manipulating digital images. He looks at images produced by others but feels he can't get the same results.

He decided to ask photographer friends to demonstrate the software they used. His most important question each time was, 'how long did it take you to learn this?' He discovered quick routes to learning, bought some entry-level software that suited his working style, catalogued his photographs, and learned how to turn basic images into great prints.

Unsung skills

You know you possess these skills, are confident using them, but you feel that most employers would put no value on them. As a result, you don't talk about these skills or try to improve them.

Example: Sue's passion is ballroom dancing, but she leaves it off her CV because she feels it's irrelevant to work. One day, she heard of a college lecturer who taught business skills through ballroom dancing. Formal dancing teaches timing, responsiveness, leading and following, reading signals, anticipating change, and paying attention to personal space. Sue realised that using these skills at work was what made her a brilliant PA.

We often think of skills like this as 'hobby skills'. They could include horticulture, craft skills, fine hand-to-eye coordination, being good at crosswords, being a great sports coach. Job-changers often say, 'I talk to my friends about this stuff all the time, but I don't know how to fit this kind of stuff into my CV or talk about it at interview'.

Example: Sally has held a number of voluntary roles, connected with school, church, and Scouting. In the past ten years she has acted as treasurer, leader, resource manager, transport coordinator, catering manager, and team leader. She condenses this into a throwaway phrase on her CV: 'voluntary interests'.

This category often includes so-called 'soft' skills. Many have a skewed idea of the business world: hard skills are seen as relevant, soft skills as 'nice to have' or ten-a-penny. The paradox, of course, is that some of the most difficult tasks are achieved through well-crafted soft skills such as careful persuading, influencing, and negotiating. Yet many candidates are worried that their 'soft' skills don't have a place in today's workplace.

Look for those moments when you say 'things just happened . . . it all came together at the last minute'. Who made it come together? If it was you, how did you do it? The clue for a skill that has value is that something changed because of your involvement. Ask someone who saw the event what it was you did, and then think about how you can build on that experience. If the skill is valuable to you, reveal its value to others. Make better connections between the skills you love using outside work and what you do 9 to 5.

Unfulfilled skills

Your unfulfilled skills are the things you'd love to do. *Listen to those dreams calling you:* I always wanted to . . . paint watercolours, ride a horse, write my autobiography, run a soup kitchen, build my own house . . .

How do we turn these fantasy scenarios into real opportunities? Don't take them at face value – interrogate them for clues about real-world career paths. For example, if you've always fancied being a long-distance lorry driver, this probably says something about enjoying freedom and independence. Sometimes the fantasy is a simple invitation. If you've always dreamed of being a novelist, take a writing class, write the opening paragraph, read more novels. Want to be an MP? Become more active in your chosen political party. Do anything, but *do something*. The real test of longing is that the idea won't leave you alone until you do something about it. The crunch comes when impulse needs to translate into action.

Watch for activities that quite literally fill your dreams. I sailed as a boy, not particularly well. I often dreamt about sailing again, and in the dream I usually felt I had no idea what I was doing. At the age of 40, I took up sailing again, and because I had practised sailing so often in my head, I was actually better at it. I've heard this phenomenon called 'learning to ski in the summer, learning to swim in the winter'. Sports research reveals that training by visualising events is almost as powerful as real experience. If that's true, then imagined skills are more powerful than you think.

Nothing is as damaging as a ruthless policy of ignoring your unfulfilled skills. Try a job on a short-term basis. Work for nothing just to get the feel of it. Shadow someone doing the job to find out if it's what you'd really like to do. Take a short course rather than a three-year degree.

Unpolished skills

Unpolished skills are skills you have identified, but you have settled for competence when you know you are capable of far more.

Example: Maya learned through her job in customer services to deal with complaints, and when to refer difficult calls to managers. She had learned the job inside out, but hated any change: new products, new support services. She had failed to stretch herself, to see what she was really capable of, because she had never looked at the underlying master skill: *keeping customers happy*. Once Maya learned to develop that skill, to invent new ways of helping people, she began to grow and was promoted to supervisor.

Example: When you learn to swim, you begin by thinking of it as organised movement. Somewhere, you think, there's a special combination of movements that will keep me above water and move me forward. The barely competent swimmer achieves that, and no more. *That'll do. I can swim.* Bill broke through that stage when he realised that swimming wasn't about movement or power, but a form of guided floating. With that idea in mind, he progressed to swimming several lengths. Then he discovered that it was also about timed breathing. Control the timing and breathing, and you can continue swimming just like you can continue walking. The first skill breakthrough will rarely be the last.

What if I don't get much out of the skills I use?

The biggest insight comes from seeing skills you excel at but don't enjoy using. If you are in demand for these skills, you may learn to love them, but you'll probably need to find ways of stretching yourself. People who dislike what they do have often hit a flat patch on their learning curve. If not, it could be that you feel the skill is not worth using (look at Exercise 9.2 – Revealing your values, p. 114).

Alternatively, say 'no' to unfulfilling tasks more often, and negotiate opportunities to use skills you enjoy. If you really can't reshape your current job (don't give up at the first attempt), perhaps it's time to move on.

Exercise 7.2 – Skill clips

If your life is a movie, when you talk about yourself in a job search you've got to decide on just a few frames. Movies are promoted through trailers – the whole plot condensed into just 2 minutes. The **skill clips** exercise sends you back to the cutting room to create a condensed, all-action version of you.

In the movie of your life, what are the key moments? Your best action scenes are the ones where you're doing things, getting results, interacting with people, starting or finishing projects.

Home movie rules for editing and composing your skill clips include:

1. **Zoom in as tight as possible** – avoid long sequences. One day is good. One hour is better. Keep it concise. Like a movie clip, it's got to convey a lot in a short space of time.
2. **Use slow motion** – reveal the action as it happens by thinking about what you did and how you did it.
3. **Use a good screenplay** – does this scene convey a message about skills, about overcoming obstacles?
4. **Keep the star in shot** – make sure this scene is about the hero: you.
5. **Make sure the clip has a happy ending** – an achievement or a skill revelation.

Fix on one event. Start with an occasion when you felt a great sense of success or achievement. Picture your 'clip', and give it a title. Then ask yourself the following skill discovery questions:

What obstacles did I have to overcome?	What did I have to do to achieve this?
What was the task or challenge?	How did I work with others?
What planning did I need to do?	What was my best moment?
What skills did I see myself use?	How did I surprise myself or others?
What skills did others see me use?	What did I do personally?

Prompts for your skill clips include:

- Think of times when you achieved something you are proud of. This doesn't need to be a work-related achievement. How did you do it? What difference did you make? Turn the event over in your mind until you see the skills you used.
- Think about work-related clips that demonstrate the full range of skills outlined earlier in the chapter.
- Now look at your achievements outside work – times in the past when you overcame the odds, did something that surprised you.

Keep drawing up these skill clips, either alone or with a fellow career developer. If you show a series of movie clips from the work of famous director Alfred Hitchcock, you see similarities of style and content. After five or six skill clips, you'll start to notice a pattern of skills, or a set of *master skills,* and you'll get a strong sense of what you are really good at *and* enjoy doing.

Example skill clip			
TITLE: **'Top of the world'**			
INTRODUCTION: I've always been frightened of heights. I was pretty unfit. My work team challenged me to climb Cwm Clogwyn in Snowdonia.			
[*Scenes*] **Opening shot:** **The problem**	**First step**	**Main action**	**Ending**
Panic! Fear of failing. Sponsorship for a good cause convinced me to go ahead	Weighing up the problem. Deciding what I needed to learn and practise	Setting off – the real thing. Putting theory and training into practice. Scary!	I made it! Photograph at the summit. Elation
Skills I used Recognising my limitations. Overcoming fear	***Skills I used*** Learning from friends, practising on a climbing wall. Learning to climb and belay, understanding equipment. Risk management? Anticipating and measuring problems	***Skills I used*** Working as a team, learning to rely on others. Responding (fast!) to instructions. Helping others to cope with their fear. Keeping people's spirits up with humour!	***Skills I used*** Celebrating – enjoying what we had achieved as a team, and my special role in our success. Reflecting on what I had managed by overcoming fear and relying on my colleagues. Insight: new ways of working together

Express achievements as mini-narratives

Communicate skills and linked achievements as concise stories (see 'Telling Tales' in Chapter 16). When you talk about your best skills, use the structure outlined below: outline the problem, talk briefly about what you did, and state the outcome.

Story: Beginning	Middle	End
The problem My company needed to simplify its accounting system and save money	*What I did* Identified, researched, and introduced an off-site central accounting function	*The outcome* 25% savings, and the new accounts centre came online to budget and on deadline

Exercise 7.3 – Motivated skills

What skills do you really enjoy using? Think about a time you were so engrossed in a task that you lost all track of time – moments when you felt completely yourself.

Look at skills you have identified in Exercise 7.1. Put them into a grid as below:

Your motivated skills	Skills I love using	Skills I quite enjoy using	Skills I don't enjoy using
Skills I perform well			
Skills I perform reasonably well but need to develop			
Skills I do not perform well			

Skills in the darker areas are those you should probably be using and developing. How many of these skills do you use in your current role?

Exercise 7.4 – Skills clock

Go back to your list of skills in Exercise 7.1. Pick out 12 skills you enjoy using. Put each skill at one of the points of a **skills clock** as below:

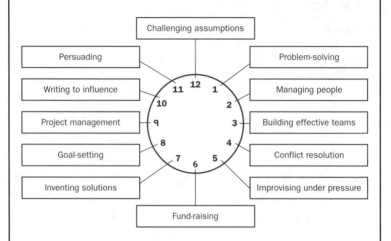

Try combining skills at different points of the clock face. Ask yourself, 'When have I used these two skills together? What sort of work would benefit from a combination of these two skills?' You might, for example, combine 2 (*Managing people*) and 7 (*Inventing solutions*). This might mean inventing new management systems, devising new ways of looking at management issues, such as giving people the tools to solve their own problems.

Combining 12 *Challenging assumptions* with 6 *Fund-raising* might make you think about turning the whole idea of fund-raising on its head. You might look at the question, 'How can we persuade more people to give us money?' and turn it around: 'How can we get people to persuade us to take their money?' Your fund-raising campaign may find a way of empowering people to select charities that exactly match their values.

'Must do' list

✓ Discover your hidden skills. Enlist the help of a good listener and talk through times when you were motivated to work.

✓ Look at the connections between your interests and the skills you love using. There's a magic combination somewhere.

✓ Try at least four skill clips. Write out the skills you discover. Look at the skills that keep coming up time and again.

✓ Look at skills you can use and combine. Make this part of your wish list in terms of what you want to do next. Put your top skills on the **Master Sheet** (see p. 261).

✓ Identify achievements for the different stages of your career.

✓ Practise talking about your skills in a way that sounds interesting rather than pushy.

Further help to identify your skills and achievements

The **JLA Skill Cards** give you an opportunity to identify and understand your top skills – not just the things
you're good at, but the skills which give you most energy.
Currently in its fourth edition, this card sort is popular
with both job hunters and coaches. The cards allow you
to choose from a comprehensive and up-to-date range
of skills valued in today's workplace. Exercises are provided so you end up with a list of your motivated skills
and linked achievement stories.

The cards come with a full set of instructions and exercises to provide achievement evidence for your CV and
job interviews, plus advice on communicating skill evidence to employers. See **www.johnleescareers.com** or
search for 'JLA Skill Cards' on **Amazon.co.uk.**

For further tips on communicating your skills at interview, see *Knockout Interview.*

Your House of Knowledge

'One need not be a Chamber – to be Haunted –
One need not be a House –
The Brain has Corridors – surpassing
Material Place –'
Emily Dickinson

This chapter helps you to:

- Tap your hidden knowledge
- Understand how your preferred interests provide huge clues about career satisfaction
- Make new connections between what you know and what you can do.

What do you choose to know about?

Knowledge is pumped into us for a great deal of the time when in full-time education, and again when we get to work. We learn things because someone else tells us they're important.

From the age of 14 or so we begin to make choices about our academic subjects. Inside and outside work, we find that some subject areas are more stimulating than others. We choose what we want to know more about. Just as we all have hidden skills, we also have concealed areas of knowledge. What's powerful about your knowledge is not just what you know, but *why* you know it. The subjects we read, learn, and think about in our own time tell us a huge amount about the things we want to put at the centre of life, the topics, ideas, people, technologies, and brands we consider to be vitally important.

Perhaps there are new areas of knowledge you have yet to discover? Work may open those doors to learning. There will almost certainly also be things you know about that you think have no relevance to work – areas of study that don't appear anywhere on your CV. Or should they?

Exercise 8.1 – House of Knowledge

This exercise helps you to identify the things you know about. It will help you to record interests that may provide links to potential work sectors. What you choose to learn about is a vital part of who you are.

What do you know about? In answering that question, people usually talk about expertise they use at work, or what they have studied. This is merely scratching the surface.

Look at the multi-storey house shown below. It has a ground floor, first floor, and second floor. It has an attic and a basement, and a garage at the side. Each level of the house represents an area of knowledge.

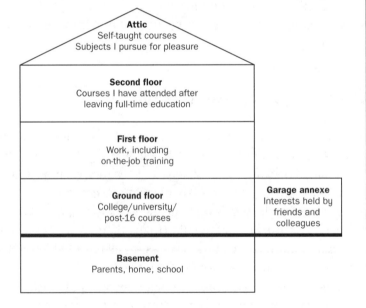

Like most exercises in this book, this works better if you have a conversation with someone while you are doing the exercise, or as soon as you have completed it.

1. Begin with the **basement** of your house, the firm foundations provided by your home and school. The following questions will help:

   - What did you learn from your parents? What was your favourite subject at school?
   - What projects or activities engaged you outside the classroom?
   - What was the first thing you wanted to read when you put aside your textbooks? What was that about?
   - When were you so enthusiastic about a subject at school or college that you went off and found more to read in your own time?

2. Complete the list for the **ground, first,** and **second floors.** Think of knowledge areas which do not yet appear in your CV – including the things you forgot you know about. Here are some prompts:

   - What training courses have you attended which you found stimulating? Think about (a) courses you chose to put yourself on and (b) courses you were sent on that turned out to be more interesting than you expected. What was the topic?
   - What subjects led you to turning points in your life (that night school in Photoshop that made you change degree course, for example)?
   - What subjects have you enjoyed training others in?
   - When in your career were you hungry to extend your learning?

3. Now think about your leisure activities and interests. This is your **attic,** the part of your brain where you store all that old junk you've forgotten you have, stuff you never thought you would find a use for. What areas of knowledge are hidden in those dusty trunks? Some prompts again:

   - When did you teach yourself something or learn something just for your own amusement?
   - When do you find yourself reading, talking or thinking about a subject and others have to shut you up? When do you find yourself so engrossed in an article or a book that the time passes unnoticed?
   - Given a free choice, what subjects would you choose to talk about over a relaxed meal?

- Think of a time when you have enjoyed learning about some- one else's favourite subject or hobby. What was the subject?
- Which internet pages do you have bookmarked at home?
- If you could teach a workshop on any subject in the world, to any audience, and given unlimited preparation time, what would that subject be?
- If you could learn about any subject in the world, from any teacher, what would that subject be?
- If you were accidentally locked into a large bookshop for the weekend, in which section would you camp out? Once you got bored, where would you go next? And next? Write down the headings displayed on the bookshelves.
- When your Sunday newspaper arrives, fat with different sec- tions, which part do you turn to first? Which part second?
- If you received a bequest from an aged relative that would fund a return to full-time education, what would you study?
- If you won the lottery and didn't have to work, you'd spend a year or two indulging yourself, but eventually you would get bored. What might you want to learn about to fill the time?

4. Look also at the **garage.** It's on the side of the house because it represents other people's strong interests. My close friend Peter Maybank has a long-held interest in the First World War. I've joined him on battlefield trips to both Verdun and the Somme, revealing what can be shaped by other people's enthusiasm.

Look at your complete house. What have you missed out? It'll prob- ably be things you consider 'trivial', such as cooking, homemaking or family history. If you enjoy it, include it. Try to remember all the things you have *chosen to know about*.

Knowledge that won't leave you in peace

The attic of the House of Knowledge potentially reveals more about us than any other part of the building. This is where we store away the special projects, the things that call to us from time to time and just won't go away.

I have had the opportunity to work alongside some very talented professional photographers. While they're clearing away, I usually ask: 'Do you still enjoy photography when you're not doing it for a living?' This is where I discover the themes and projects closest to each photographer's heart. Cheshire-based Richard Weston (Weston Digital Imaging) has a personal project which has already become an award-winning portfolio, documenting his son's work as a drag artist. Colin McPherson gave me a postcard illustrating his long-term work documenting the last salmon net fishermen on the east coast of Scotland.

Chapter 11 discusses how people can feel 'called' to certain roles. A very common piece of career advice is 'follow your passion' – suggesting you should build a career around your strongest interest. This idea has its flaws. The website 80000hours.org looked at over 60 studies of what makes a 'dream job' and found that the idea of 'following your passion' can lead you astray. Steve Jobs was a keen follower of Zen Buddhism before entering technology, and Condoleezza Rice was a talented classical musician before she started studying politics. The website argues that we can develop a 'passion' for any work that we find enjoyable and meaningful, and job satisfaction needs multiple ingredients: being engaged by varied and stimulating tasks; helping other people; using motivated skills; having supportive colleagues; being treated well by an organisation and avoiding major negatives such as job insecurity; and, finally, a role that fits your personal life.

Focusing just on what you feel passionate about ignores the facts that there are many elements to any role, motivations change, and we can develop new interests in life. Additionally, the mantra to 'follow your passion' often persuades you that there's no point exploring until the perfect job comes along.

Even so, don't ignore strong interests. They may not map exactly onto your work role, but they provide important clues about potential sectors. For example, if your spare time joy is building boats, you may not want to do this for a living because it wouldn't pay enough and would ignore other skills. However, the amateur boat-builder might investigate options for working in craft-related sectors, construction, boat sales or supplies, or shipping (see Chapter 10 on identifying sectors). The things you love to know about can provide powerful signposts towards exciting work sectors, and the motivation to explore them more deeply.

'Must do' list

- ✓ Show your completed house to a friend. Talk about the activities in your past which filled you with energy. Where is that energy today?
- ✓ If you've caught yourself saying 'ah, I really used to enjoy . . .', then look at why you dropped the activity or interest. Is there a 'yes, but' in there somewhere?
- ✓ What can you add to your CV in terms of knowledge?
- ✓ What career ideas are prompted by information from any part of the house?
- ✓ What ideas are suggested by the subjects in the attic of your house?
- ✓ What career ideas are you going to investigate further?

Personality fit

'It is absurd to divide people into good and bad.
People are either charming or tedious'.
Oscar Wilde

This chapter helps you to:

- See how personality and work are connected
- Identify your working style
- Spot contexts and roles where your personality fits
- Anticipate psychometric testing
- Gain insights into your values and how you apply them at work.

Personality type

Personality type is broadly connected with career choice – but the word *broadly* should be emphasised. If you're a 'people person', you will probably choose an occupation that allows you to work with others, but this could be in a very wide range of work sectors. Equally, quiet people can work for organisations which are full of outgoing people. So, given the wide range of sectors you might work in with any personality, it's perhaps best to focus on areas of comfort and discomfort.

Your personality in the workplace

Work role. If the majority of the tasks you undertake are a good match to your temperament, work generally fits well. For example, if you love the opportunity to perform detailed work and that's exactly what you're hired to do, the working day may be well balanced. If you find yourself constantly outside your comfort zone, that's a fair indication that your personality doesn't suit your work.

Using the right **skills** can be related to personality. Doing things well and enjoying what you do may feed your self-esteem. A mismatch between your motivated skills (see Chapter 7) and your work role can easily make you feel under-appreciated.

Your personality provides strong clues about the kind of **team** you would work best in. Look at past team experiences to work out what your natural role is in any team – Leader? Diplomat? Go-getter?

Career drivers have strong links to personality (see Chapter 6). Compare your main drivers to what your job requires of you. Look at past roles as well – how is your work performance changed by being in a role that more closely matches your hot buttons?

Where your **values** are matched in work, you may feel you're doing something meaningful, and your small part of the world is improved by the fact that you're doing it. Alternatively, if you feel there is something missing, it may be that your role is hollow: productive on the outside, but empty at its core (see Exercise 9.2).

Personality also links strongly with the kind of **boss** you will work best with. How do you feel about being micromanaged? How important is it to have a boss who trusts you to get on with the job and supports you even if you make the odd mistake?

Do you respond best to a small **organisation** that offers variety and challenge and often needs you to be self-reliant, or are you happier in the more defined structure of a larger organisation? Do you feel constrained by small organisations? Or by being an anonymous cog in a large business?

Working conditions can affect mood and commitment in some personality types. How far is your motivation affected by the following: location, travel, the kind of building you work in, what you can see from your office window, where you spend your lunch hour?

Self-esteem often comes out of **opportunities for learning**. Does your job keep stretching you? What have you learned in the past 12 months? Who sets your learning agenda? For some, growth is linked to **advancement**. Is your present role a useful stepping-stone to the future? Do you have a clear plan for the next five years? Do you need one? How would a recruiter see your present role: as a dead end, a side alley, or a building block in your career?

People often seek different kinds of **pace** and **challenge** at work. Do you prefer to be constantly facing new problems, or do you need time to deal with the work you're given and to process new ideas? Does rapid change fill you with energy, or do you find it threatening? Does your organisation make things happen quickly enough for you? Are you being pushed to work at a speed that feels uncomfortable? How do you feel about leaving things half completed?

Getting a handle on your personality

Exercise 9.1 offers some broad indicators about your personality. There are no 'right' answers. Put a score on each scale, avoiding the midpoint. Think about the way you see yourself, the way others see you, and the way you react under pressure. Increased self-awareness will provide good clues about your best fit in terms of people and organisational culture.

After completing the chart, ask someone who knows you well to judge how far you have produced an accurate self-portrait.

Exercise 9.1 – Personality Overview

How would you describe yourself? Place a tick on each scale.

Confident   Cautious

Head in the clouds   Practical

Abstract   Concrete

Logical   Intuitive

Emotional   Analytical

Optimistic   Pessimistic

Open to change   Reluctant to change

Self-reliant   Need the approval of others

Emotionally vulnerable   Self-assured

Follower   Leader

Solo artist   Team player

Steady   Flexible

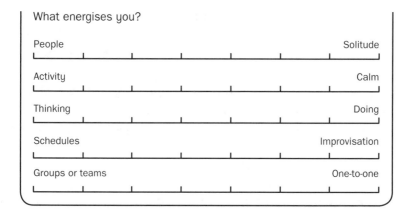

Go with the grain

TV programmes about career change often show partici-
pants being encouraged to 'fake it' – to bluff, claiming skills
and experience they don't possess. This has little connection with reality. Selection processes gather information
carefully, scrutinising candidates' backgrounds.

However, you might be tempted to mask aspects of your
personality. This is usually based on the assumption that
only one personality style is acceptable. You'll hear colleagues say, for example, 'I really need to be more assertive'.
Similarly, people believe that they aren't smart enough to be
offered a job. Intelligence is often considered just in terms of
IQ scores, or success in passing examinations.

Psychologists argue that intelligence has many forms.
Some people are good with language, some with numbers,
visual images, logic, music; others have highly developed
physical skills and awareness. Others may have no qualifications but have practical common sense and problem-solving
capacity. Some have highly developed 'people skills', others
are better at tasks requiring quiet reflection. In other words,
people are 'smart' in different kinds of ways.

Don't beat yourself up for not being someone else; recognise your strengths. Identify the contexts where you work at your best, and seek them out. It's like working with a piece of wood – life is much easier if you go with the grain. Stop believing you need to be someone else, and start celebrating the way *you* are. Of course, at interview, it's good to present the best version of *you* – what you are like on a good day.

Personality tests and questions

During an interview, you may face questions about how closely you match the job, but also questions that seem to have very little connection to job content at all. Questions about personality can sound vague or off the wall, but an employer is trying to assess how team members will react to you, and how you will relate to the wider world, including customers.

Start by imagining what kind of personality will do well in the role. That's the picture you need to match. Think about whether your CV evidence and interview answers will confirm or undermine this picture. Show rather than tell. Rather than make empty claims like 'I work well under pressure', give examples. Prepare answers like this for all key personality characteristics you can spot on the employer's shopping list. Rehearse strong mini-narratives that convey useful all-round strengths like flexibility, working with difficult people, overcoming problems, or getting things done with thin resources.

You may meet psychometric tests in a selection process. These vary from ability tests, including numerical and verbal reasoning tests, to personality tests. The Myers–Briggs Type Indicator (MBTI) is used widely in staff development, but has its critics because it is based on Jungian type theory.

More recent instruments (for example, OPQ and 16PF5) give results based on the 'big five' traits. Tests of this nature should be conducted by a qualified practitioner – see the useful British Psychological Society guide (2017).

Where you've undergone personality testing, you may be asked in more detail about your working style, particularly if the test results suggest that you might not be an ideal fit. Again, have some good examples up your sleeve and show that you're capable of adapting to a wide range of circumstances.

When going through a selection process, you may be asked to take a psychometric test of some kind. I couldn't think of anyone better than my colleague Peter Fennah, Chartered Psychologist, to explain the process:

Personality tests – what to expect from an assessment process

You will be asked to complete a personality questionnaire (untimed), typically completing it online before you attend the assessment centre. At the same time, you are likely to be asked to complete standard numerical, verbal, and abstract ability questions, though these would be under timed conditions of between 6 to 25 minutes each. There will be a couple of example questions to complete to ensure you fill the form in correctly (pay attention here if you know you get easily distracted). Ensure you are relaxed and distraction-free. Ideally, you should seek to complete each exercise in one sitting taking a break between activities – if you have to stop part way through or lose your internet connection, your answers are likely to have been saved up until this point, so you shouldn't lose more than a few answers and can pick it up again from where you left off.

For ability questionnaires, don't expect to answer the same questions as other candidates you know who have completed even the same assessment. Test publishers draw on a large bank of questions and have automated systems to mix up the actual questions.

The reason you may be asked to complete a personality questionnaire as part of the recruitment process is to determine your likely fit for the role/team, your response to the pressures of performing the role, and operating within the culture of the organisation. At this point you may be thinking of how to skew your answers to match what the employer wants to hear. There are three risks to this. First, psychologists designing robust personality questionnaires include measures to check the consistency of your answers and compare them to other population groups. This reveals exaggerated responses which will be probed at interview. Being 'found out' in this way can be uncomfortable and unhealthy for your career. Second, if you are a poor fit for some parts of the role but your performance on the other elements of the assessment process is good, the employer would normally want to talk about effective coping strategies to help you perform to your best in the role. If you have skewed your answers, then this conversation has little value. Third, no one is a perfect match. Every person will shape the role around their strengths so it is better to be authentic, work with the way you are, and attempt to make a success of the role. If you really are a wrong match, then it is far better for both you and the employer to know this early; another role may be available that would suit you better.

Employers following best practice will provide you with detailed feedback on your psychometric results. This may partly be through a report document, but ideally you should also have around 30 minutes with a trained professional who will discuss your results and check that they have been interpreted accurately. Psychometric tools are not perfect and there can be a lot of legitimate reasons for different results to emerge. Therefore, if there are any surprises in the results, it is good to explore these. This is why trained professionals play a key role in the feedback and assessment process.

Peter Fennah is a Chartered and Registered Occupational Psychologist and accredited executive coach. He focuses upon developing agile leadership and aiding those in career transition. Visit www. careersynergy.com

Values

The word 'values' is horribly over-used today, often describing the way organisations want us to believe they behave. Values language is most powerful when it influences behaviours and how people are treated. Sometimes we recognise our values most clearly when they are challenged, such as the customer service manager who is required to make false promises and lie to customers.

Values are therefore not just words – they are principles we live out. They are judged by outcomes, and when actions and words match, we see authenticity. Knowing the difference between value statements and embedded values matters when it comes to choosing employers. Most organisations celebrate and publish their values. They say that they believe in their staff and customers and take care of the environment. How far these words translate into concrete actions varies immensely. Part of your due diligence as a job hunter is to tell the difference between organisations that engage in spin, and those that make a reasonable effort to put their stated values into practice.

We take our values to work, and judge our work by its closeness to those values. Sometimes you might be asked to do something you think is dishonest or unfair. You might witness behaviours or language you do not admire. What were your values when you began your career? How have they changed, and why? Where have your values been affirmed at work, and where have they been questioned, challenged, or flattened?

Exercise 9.2 – Revealing your values

Step 1 – Values seen in others

People often reveal their values in the way they behave. What behaviours and attitudes do you **dislike**? (Some words to start you thinking: *judgemental, intolerant, lazy, arrogant*.)

What behaviours and attitudes do you **admire most**? (Some words to start you thinking: *modest, honest, self-sacrificing, caring, creative, brave, encouraging, ethical, reliable, consistent*.)

Step 2 – Where your values have been challenged

Sometimes we may feel that work is in conflict with our personal values. For example:

- You were asked to do something you didn't believe in.
- You observed behaviours or language you don't feel comfortable with.
- You were asked to behave in a way that clashes with your personal values.

Think of **a day at work** where you were in a situation which did NOT match your values. Record your answers below.

What happened?
Why did the event challenge your values?
Based on this event, how would you describe your values?

Step 3 – Organisational values

Think about organisations you know well, including ones you have worked for. What values do you admire most in these organisations?

Results of this exercise

You can use this information in a number of ways. You can look for shared values in a team you might be joining, and you can investigate those organisations and sectors where your values might be matched.

'Must do' list

Questions to help you reflect on your personality and working style:

- ✓ What brings you to life? When or where do you become energised? What has a deadening effect on you?
- ✓ What work environments suit you best? What kind of intelligence do you bring to the workplace?
- ✓ How far might your next career step require you to work on self-awareness, resilience, or improved interpersonal skills?
- ✓ How well can you anticipate what a psychometric test will reveal about you?
- ✓ What preparation do you need to answer questions on how you operate under pressure, or your strengths and weaknesses?
- ✓ What are your values, and what kind of work would match them best?

10

Choosing your world

'So many out-of-the-way things had happened lately,
that Alice had begun to think that very few things
indeed were really impossible'.
Lewis Carroll

This chapter helps you to:

- Understand work sectors
- Find out about kinds of work you know nothing about at present
- Map out sectors that you would like to research
- Use lateral thinking to help you to identify new sectors and connections between them
- Begin active investigation.

Choices

Think of the billions of people who have lived on this planet throughout history, and the nearly eight billion who live on it today. According to some calculations, about one in ten of all the people who ever lived are alive right now. The reason is obvious – there are more of us, and we're living longer. This 10% slice of humanity has more choices available to it than any previous generation. Your great-grandparents probably had no more than ten obvious jobs to choose from.

Today, there are tens of thousands of occupations available. However, we're still using the same choice-making brain as every previous generation.

Putting experience into compartments

When a kindly uncle asks his six-year-old niece 'What do you want to do when you grow up?', the answer is supposed to be a job title. We're expected to choose the right label from an early age, without knowing much about work. Later in life, in social situations, you're asked 'What do you do?', looking again for the same, simplified label. We'd get different results asking about someone's working mix (see Exercise 3.2 – Your Jigsaw Job, p. 39).

Society likes to put ideas into boxes. This begins at school. You didn't have classes entitled *Thinking*, *Speaking*, *Imagination*, or *Wisdom* (you might have done if we still followed Renaissance ideas about education). In the Victorian age, educators reclassified what was taught into narrower boxes (and at the same time invented new subjects, including English and Physics).

The problem is that these classroom subjects *seem* to point towards career paths. This 'educational funnelling' limits early career thinking. We encourage young people to narrow down their subject choices (for example, choosing around four subjects at A-level and then one primary subject at university), and this sets up a false expectation that these decisions helpfully narrow down career choices. However, few degree subjects outside science and technology *directly* relate to the jobs graduates perform. Every year we turn out thousands of newly qualified people who have no idea how to make their qualifications relevant to employers (see Chapter 18).

The way we link study to work is often limiting. If you're good at languages, you'll think about being a translator, teaching, or possibly working in export/import. Beyond that you may run out of ideas. If you're a child who is good at music, art, or drama, well-meaning relatives will doubtless remind you of the fact that creative artists often struggle to make a living. Options close down quickly, and soon you're drifting towards 'sensible' subjects and jobs, even though these routes are less exciting. If you're good with numbers, written or spoken communication, or computer applications, choices broaden. Few school subjects have a direct link to sectors – there are few people practising 'pure' geography, history, or mathematics in the world, and there are many top-level generalists. How do you know where you might fit into the world of work?

Sectors – and choosing them more carefully

One way of thinking about the many types of jobs in the world is to categorise them – sort them into groups. Imagine an office block full of filing cabinets. Every type of job in the world you can imagine, from Aardvark Handler to Zebra Painter, has its own file in one of those cabinets. To make sense of this huge range of roles, you might group related files together in one room. Thus we cluster jobs together. Sometimes these groupings are known as job families or fields of work; here we call them *sectors*. Some sectors are huge, such as health, education, or engineering. Others are niche, tiny, or brand new.

Sectors are powerful because they often connect you with activities that feel purposeful and interesting, and people who value similar things to you and, metaphorically, speak the same language. Working with products, technologies, brands, or people who inspire you often leads straightforwardly to job satisfaction.

Talk to people who love their work, and you often hear them say 'it's a great industry' – they enjoy their sector. These are people who seem very happy to talk about their work even when they're not working. Once you find a sector that gives you the same 'buzz', you will approach both your job search and the work you do far more positively. The spin-offs, both for yourself and for any organisation which employs you, are important:

- You will be more enthusiastic at interviews – and employers love enthusiasm.
- You will enjoy passing on knowledge to colleagues, and so improve your visibility.
- You will find it easier to fit into an organisation which does things you believe are valuable.
- You will be motivated to keep learning.

It's common among career changers to hear them say, 'I would really like to work in a sector which inspires me, but I will find it much easier to get a job in the sector I have been working in for the last 20 years'. It's easy to choose a sector that's familiar, or one that seems 'safe'.

Resources for investigation

How do we discover what sectors exist, and what it's like to work in them? In the past we had to rely on careers libraries, but today a wealth of information is a mouse click away. Investigate sectors and jobs using comprehensive sites (start with prospects.ac.uk). Research organisations within sectors, noting the titles of jobs you see mentioned. Check out online video interviews (for example, careersbox. co.uk) where people talk about their jobs. You can also find out about organisation cultures and job satisfaction levels. Websites such as www.glassdoor.com can be a good starting point for learning about why people leave or stay. However, remember that opinions from former workers are often negative. Check out a range of opinions, and make sure they're up to date and supported by your own investigation.

Discovering what enlivens, and what dampens

If you're unhappy at work, one reason may be the people you work with. It may be environmental: you don't like your place of work or the journey that takes you there. These can all alter (change of boss, relocation) without your role changing at all. You may be out of tune with the organisation – particularly if you don't share its values (see Chapter 9).

Some people are happy in their role no matter which sector they work in. Would you enjoy doing the role you do in a different sector? Someone who enjoys networking computers, for example, probably doesn't mind doing the job in a factory, hospital, or office building. Others are dissatisfied with work – but don't realise that they haven't yet found a sector which feels interesting.

Problems you will encounter when choosing sectors

Problem 1: Not knowing what's out there

Choosing from unknown careers is like trying to plan a journey using a road atlas full of blank pages. Sector discovery helps you draw missing maps.

If you can't find a sector that suits you, then you may have to find a new angle. Work is changing so rapidly that new disciplines are being created all the time. Maybe you'll dream up an entirely new sector. Before Galileo, there really wasn't a discipline you could describe as experimental physics. The word 'scientist' wasn't invented until the 1830s. Before Freud, there wasn't a sector called psychoanalysis. The world wide web was made available to the public in 1991, but took several years to become established. The internet as we know it today has transformed the way we work and creates new kinds of jobs every week, and it's still a new phenomenon. Something that has transformed society has only been around, in human terms, for a heartbeat.

Discover the way sectors are changing fast, and look for new ideas, new organisations, new approaches and technologies.

Problem 2: Second-hand information

A huge amount we know about sectors is tainted, sometimes by bias. Information is filtered by other people's experiences and the opinions of family, colleagues, and friends. When people describe jobs, they attach value tags (safe/risky, dull/exciting, boring/cutting edge, fixed/changing). Sometimes this information is entirely accurate, providing you with really important clues about what work is actually like. Often advice is out of date, subjective – or plain wrong.

Start with your own discoveries, not with someone else's prejudices. Don't rely on the slanted, possibly jaded views of retired professionals, recruiters, or friends – find out for yourself. One characteristic about people who have made huge, brave career changes is that they became excited about what they didn't know, and started to do something about the gap in their knowledge.

You begin to know what's out there by being fascinated by what's out there. Active exploration, not endless reflection, is the key to forward movement.

Problem 3: Choosing too narrow a range

It's easy to choose sectors that are established, and miss new, growing, or changing sectors. Watch out for a blinkered or sentimental reliance on one sector.

Let's say your interest is in forestry. You like working outdoors in the wild woods. You go through the training which adds to your depth of background knowledge about forestry and conservation. You get a job. You find yourself dealing with peripheral problems such as record-keeping, litter, or car parks. You find that less and less of your knowledge and enthusiasm is being tapped, and you are increasingly learning about regulations, funding, and government initiatives: possible career crisis. You find yourself saying, 'I came into forestry because I love conservation and wildlife, but I've become a bureaucrat'.

I hear the same story almost every week from people in teaching, HR, nursing, travel, university lecturing, and ministry. What I hear is this: 'I was attracted by the box called nursing, and I liked what it said on the label: caring for people, being there for patients and relatives. What am I now? A form filler'.

Problem 4: Exploring from a distance

Exploring sectors can look like a piece of desk research you do at home on your own. Yes, you'll uncover basic information this way, but you won't understand how it fits together, or how it feels.

Trawl for basic information online, and then decide what further questions arise. Instead of clicking from one website to another, reach for your phone. If you're shy or hesitant, start with someone easy to approach. Ask to talk to people in their place of work – or by video call. Remember that *the* great question to ask someone doing any job is this: *What do you do most of the time?*

This process is not just about gathering information – it's also about *decoding*. Hearing first-hand about top performers gives you insider knowledge of how to describe your own strengths. Decoding also helps you translate your experience so it becomes convincing to hirers. And if information and decoding weren't powerful enough, face-to-face conversations have another impact: *perception*. Being heard asking great questions ensures you're remembered; every conversation increases your visibility in the hidden job market (see Chapter 12 for the benefits of information interviews).

Problem 5: How do I know if I'll like it?

This question gives away an assumption: *the only way to really find out is to take a job and see if it works out*. It's worth reading that last sentence again. Taking a job to discover if you like it is one of the nation's favourite career strategies. Too many candidates experiment by taking a job because it looks acceptable (or it's the first one to come along).

No one should take a job knowing little about the sector or organisation. It's vital to know a great deal before an interview. Research makes you a credible candidate, but also reveals if the role fits you. Seek information, not hunches, and find out what roles are really like (for more on this process of due diligence, see *Get Ahead In Your New Job*).

This doubt about whether you'll like the job is also about confidence. Notice that moment of hesitation before you write down the name of a sector. Look at what's going on in your head: *I'll never get into this sector. I don't have the training. I don't know enough.* Self-criticism should have no part in your exploration. This stage of exploration isn't about you, but what's out there. Investigation will show you how far you match role requirements. When the time comes to win someone over at interview, that's when you manage your confidence as well as your evidence.

Problem 6: Moving on from subjects to sectors to choices

Career changers often get stuck. They identify subject areas that look fascinating, but they can't make a connection between a subject of interest (for example, history) and work sectors. They succumb too quickly to 'either/or' thinking (see Chapter 4): sectors are *either* for work *or* pleasure. Friends might suggest you 'follow this interest in your spare time'. Most of us work such long hours that spare time interests are often put on the back burner for several years. You might also be asked, 'if you do what you love for a living, won't you get sick of it?' Again this ignores the experience of all those people who describe work as an enjoyable, central part of life.

Identifying sectors that will interest and inspire you

If you can't see how you can move from subjects to potential sectors, you need to make better connections. Look back at your House of Knowledge in Chapter 8. What subjects, topics, and themes energise you? What do you love learning or talking about? What work activities are you eager to talk about at weekends? What are you hungry to know more about?

The exercises in this chapter will point you to sectors that interest you. Make sure these *are* sectors – 'consultancy' isn't a sector, but a way of working; 'management' is a function. Are your sectors too big? Look at sub-sectors. For example, if your sector is marketing, ask yourself what products or services you want to promote. What names are given to these sub-sectors and jobs inside them? Picking up the language helps for interviews and builds credibility.

Pushing sector alternatives

The ability to push for alternatives is a powerful thinking skill. The mind has a natural longing for patterns and certainty, and often wants to decide things too quickly. A training colleague had a phrase for this: 'Don't confuse me with facts, my mind is made up'. Instinctively you may worry about the randomness of your discoveries, but of course the world of work is random and fluid.

You may come up with a wide range of sector ideas. Having too many choices might seem a recipe for indecision. Use appropriate thinking tools to help you narrow things down (see Exercise 4.2 – Career Transition Diamonds, p. 50). Essentially, you are moving on from brainstorming – generating as many ideas as you can – to prioritising. Test ideas, group them together, and focus on the next step. Wherever possible, turn an idea into a question, and a question into a conversation.

Watch also for the passive mindset. Career changers love tests, boxes, and checklists. Their brain is saying, 'I feed the data in *here*, and the answer pops out *here*'. It's tempting to sit back and wait for a computer test to sample your interests and name suitable job titles. These tests don't look at the full range of things that makes a career work for you, including your personality, values, and motivated skills. Additionally, tests that generate job titles have no hope of keeping up with the wide range of jobs available. Tests should only ever be used to prompt exploration, never to dictate.

Switching sectors: the challenge

Do you want to change what you do or the sector you work in? Look at the options, and the increasing levels of difficulty:

1. It is relatively straightforward to remain in the same sector but change occupation. For example, you may remain in insurance but move from being a payroll administrator to become a learning and development specialist.

2. It is relatively straightforward to remain in the same occupation, but switch sector – for example, remain an accountant but switch from manufacturing to the hotel trade.

It's harder but not impossible to change both occupation and sector at the same time. You will need even more detailed research; find people who have done it before you. Perhaps consider a stepping-stone approach: change one element now, and another in, say, 12 months' time, when you have gained some relevant experience.

From discovery to action

Re-imagining career possibilities gives you places to look. The key next stage is *finding out*. The second half of this book provides several prompts to activity, but let's nail down one plain fact. If you want to put off career change forever (or at least until it's too late), then keep on reflect ing, analysing, and mulling over. Keep on thinking that you have to make the perfect decision before you act. That will happily prevent change. If you don't want to spend your last inactive years saying 'I wish', do something – and do it soon.

Finding out, and following your enthusiasm, costs very little. Deciding to look is a small decision. You don't need to have a perfect target job to start the process of discovery, just a sense of curiosity. And here's a big clue: any breakthrough probably has a tiny chance of happening as a result of reading or thinking, and a huge chance of coming about as a result of *other people*. Someone you already know, possibly. Or, even more likely, someone you meet in the next three months as a result of your active enquiries.

So what's the first step? Obviously, a conversation. Start with people you know, even if they seem disconnected from the world you want to enter. Find opportunities to talk to people who love what they do for a living. Experiment with REVEAL interviews (see Chapter 14).

Generating ideas for change

Look again at the sector choices prompted by various exercises in this book, and your work themes (see Exercise 5.2, p. 69). Create time to explore sectors that attract your curiosity. Don't allow 'yes, but' thinking to get in the way. You don't have to make a decision at this stage – all you're doing is generating ideas. Here are some other tried-and-tested prompts to get you to generate job ideas:

- Think of people you know who are doing interesting jobs. What's interesting about them?
- What jobs have you applied for in the past but didn't get?
- What jobs have you seen advertised that caught your attention for 30 seconds, even if you did nothing about them?

Don't get hung up on another job myth: *if you turn a hobby into a living, you will fall out of love with it.* This myth has its roots in a time when people had plenty of spare time and energy outside work for all kinds of unpaid activity. In today's 24/7 economy, it's more common to find people who work, shop, do their laundry, and get back to work.

This myth also ignores that fact that some people are paid to do things they would happily do for nothing. Starting with topics, causes, and ideas that motivate you means you work with energy. Sometimes (especially if you're going through a mid-life realignment) it's important to find things that feed the tired soul.

Exercise 10.1 – Sector match

Subjects that interest me	Obvious matching sectors	Not so obvious sectors	Wild ideas	Example organi-sations
Creative writing	Copywriting, journalism	Internal communications	Lobbying	

1. In column 1, list subjects that interest you. Use the House of Knowledge (Chapter 8) to help identify them. Add any extras that come to mind.
2. Against each subject, record at least two **obvious matching sectors** – for example, if you have put 'history' in column 1, obvious sectors for column 2 might include *museums, conservation*.
3. Now think of two or more **not so obvious sectors**, asking yourself, 'where else are people who know about this subject employed?' (e.g. *documentary making*). Do your homework (e.g. Google 'Career ideas for language learners').
4. Add any **wild ideas** that come to mind. Don't dismiss anything; be as imaginative as possible.
5. Ask friends for suggestions in all columns.
6. Research interesting new sector ideas suggested.
7. As you think of names of example organisations, list them in the right-hand column. Use these example organisations as targets for your contact list (see Exercise 14.2 – The Connections Game, p. 201).

Exercise 10.2 – Combining work ideas

1. Work on your list of sectors that interest you until you have 20 sectors. Write them out on cards or Post-it notes.
2. Redefine any phrases that are too broad (e.g. 'Management', 'Consultancy').
3. Divide your 20 cards into two piles – first choice and second choice. Your first choice pile represents sectors that you would like to have some work in during the next two years.
4. Take six sector cards from your first choice list – six sectors which particularly appeal to you. Put three in a row, and then three in a column, as below. Put a piece of paper between them and draw a 9-square grid in the empty space.

	Card 1 Physical fitness	Card 2 Language translation	Card 3 Export/import
Card 4 Creative writing			
Card 5 Health & safety			
Card 6 Ecotourism			

5. Try to come up with a sector or sub-sector to write in each blank square. A completed example is shown below:

	Card 1 Physical fitness	Card 2 Language translation	Card 3 Export/import
Card 4 Creative writing	Writing creative self-help books promoting fitness	Translating novels	Writing export guides

Card 5 Health & safety	Safety awareness in personal fitness regimes	Translation of specialised safety manage- ment texts	Exporting products and systems relating to safety management
Card 6 Ecotourism	Carbon-neutral sports events	Translating commercial tourism ideas into ecotourism	Importing ecotourism practices from another culture

6. Use these new sector ideas to prompt investigation (find out about entry routes, qualifications and training required, measures for success, prospects).

Your 'must do' guide to exploring sectors

✓ Look back at your working life. Identify sectors you have found satisfying or interesting. Why?

✓ Draw up a prioritised list of sectors that appeal to you. Set out a plan for investigation.

✓ Talk to people in jobs. Find out how they got them. Use information interviews (see Chapter 14).

✓ Become a future watcher. Read articles about how your target sectors are changing.

✓ When you've decided what you find exciting, tell people. Ask for their help.

✓ Don't allow 'yes, but' thinking to prevent further investigation of a sector that interests you.

✓ Investigate career ideas thoroughly – as if you were researching for somebody else.

✓ Use the **Master Sheet** (p. 261) to identify and list target sectors.

Changing career and finding work worth doing

'Pressed into service means pressed out of shape'.
Robert Frost

This chapter helps you to:

- Rethink the idea of 'career change'
- Look at the way we choose career paths
- Experiment with small steps and micro-projects
- Consider finding work that feels more purposeful, or more like a calling
- Take an online questionnaire to help with the process of career change.

Career change

Let's tackle head-on this whole 'change of career' notion. I argue that we have only one career – built up of multiple experiences that include work, learning, personal development, as well as the things that engage us outside work. Incidentally, you will do better at interview if you talk in these terms rather than apologising for 'changing career' or 'switching paths' or any other loaded language which implies that (a) there's only one, conventional way of having a career, (b) any progress you've made is entirely accidental, and (c) you have no idea where you're going next.

So how do you begin if you want to add more colour, more variety to your single, integrated career path? Books with the words 'interview' or 'CV' or 'job search' in the title tend to sell best, but where people really need help is with a statement like 'I have a feeling I want to do something completely different'. People ask for help partly because of the huge ranges of choices available in life.

Making a career change is much tougher than making a job change. It's a journey into the unfamiliar that will require new information, new ways of thinking, a strong CV, and well-planned interview answers. Deciding to change career increases risk: small risks of rejection, and big risks that it will all go wrong. So, confidence and learning how to make progress without burning all of your boats are both critically important.

We live in a society that likes to have lifestyle choices, and yet we are also slightly in love with the idea of the *dream job* – a role that fits perfectly and satisfies completely. Some believe that a simple career test will reveal the answer. This book will show you that 'dream' job is an idea that gets in the way. To love your work, you just need a healthy overlap between what the job needs and who you are.

Small steps

Many self-help books try to persuade you that everyone has a hidden, 'real' self, and if we can unlock this secret, then the answer to the question 'what should I do with my life?' will become crystal clear. The popular press reinforces the idea that deep down we all have a dream job, and we long for overnight transformation. That's why newspapers love stories of 'accountant becomes skydiver' or 'commando becomes nanny'.

In fact, such transformations are relatively rare. Usually people progress by gradual steps; they 'try on' careers experimentally. Many do this in their first ten years of work, when it's relatively easy to change direction and experiment. We often write off this period of our life as uncertain 'drifting'. The idea that we are more likely to make incremental than dramatic career changes was explored in depth by Herminia Ibarra (2003).

Jim Bright takes a different approach. In his book with Robert Pryor (2011), he applies chaos theory to careers work. Bright suggests that random events play an important part in career choice; we rationalise decisions in hindsight, but most were improvised responses to an unpredictable world. Jim Bright found that about three-quarters of people have changed direction because of an unplanned event. Bright argues the value of seeking out new experiences rather than trying to plan and predict (see Chapter 4 on Shift Projects, p. 53).

Making a huge leap in your career is not straightforward. This is particularly true if it involves a change of sector (for example, moving from events management to sports coaching) or a major change of lifestyle (for example, from financial director to author). It's a risky process (as people will take delight in reminding you) because it's about moving from known to unknown. It helps to begin with subjects that fascinate you. If you want breakthrough, commit time to exploring sectors of interest, keep an open mind, and try ideas on for size.

How do we choose a career?

When I have a first session with a client, I ask about past, present, and future. What has motivated this person in the past, both within work and outside it? What was the best job? The best organisation? What's going on right now that makes change attractive? Then we move to 'what next?'

Clients usually say they have no idea what they want to do, but they usually know something. I think it was the US careers specialist Richard Knowdell who stated that everyone in the world knows exactly what they should be doing. The problem, he said, is that half haven't found the words to describe what they're looking for. The other half know exactly what they should be doing but are too frightened to say it.

As Chapter 10 revealed, we are funnelled into sectors of work by academic choices. However, many influences shape our career choices.

People and other influences in career choice

- **Parental expectations** – occupational groups tend to repeat themselves in families.
- **Parental aspirations** – young people are directed towards careers that match what parents believe to be the right kind of work.
- **Academic subjects** – what you choose to study may seem like the key to your future.
- **Money and status** – academic high-achievers are often pushed towards high-pay, high-status occupations such as law, finance, or medicine.
- **Peer pressure** – doing something cool; avoiding things that look boring.
- **Advice from your first boss** – the opinion of your first manager often shapes the way you plan your career.
- **Personal values and beliefs** – the kind of work that seems worthwhile.
- **Media influence** – the jobs we see done on TV or in films or on YouTube.

- **Teachers and lecturers** – because of the effect of educational 'funnelling'.
- **High visibility** – jobs you see around you a great deal of the time.
- **Careers advisers** – particularly influential while you are also making study choices.
- **Work-related tests** – ranging from *bona fide* personality or interest inventories to something you found on the internet.
- **Personal inclination** – your strong (or vague) sense of what might work, what you are 'supposed' to be doing, or what you feel called to in life.

The first item above, parental expectations, is more influential than you might think – occupations often repeat themselves in families. We gravitate towards jobs that touch our lives. If you spend a lot of time in hospital in childhood, you may want to be a nurse or a doctor. In a TV programme about a remote Indian Ocean island that lacked even a school or post office, a young boy was asked what he wanted to do when he grew up. *Fishing*, he said, naming the one job he could see available to adult males.

Work on screen

Even in our developed society, we are exposed to only a fraction of the jobs available. Do you know what a systems analyst does, or a risk assessor, or a music therapist? New types of jobs are created every day.

Some jobs are more visible than others. You know what a surgeon, a barrister, or a firefighter does. Well, you *think* you do, but how much of your perception is based on what you see on TV? Some jobs are never off the screen (medics, lawyers, teachers, police officers, CSIs, chefs), others shown rarely (when did you see TV fiction include an offshore rigger, 3D designer, personal shopper, car valeter, or order picker?). Some occupations in the same sector are given very different weighting: TV loves architects but tends to ignore surveyors.

Television samples jobs, showing us a limited and distorted picture of work. When you see a police officer on TV, in fiction or in a documentary, you usually see someone chasing and apprehending a criminal. Talk to a police officer yourself and you discover that even those on the 'beat' spend most of their time doing one thing: responding to emails. TV prefers the more exciting moments: the airline pilot avoiding a crash, the lawyer bringing in a surprise witness, the medic diagnosing a mystery illness.

What would you do if . . .

The great benefit of 'what if . . .' questions is they allow you to put the dangerous word 'realistic' aside for a moment. Rather than trying to make a decision, you look at varying possibilities and the changes they might bring.

Ask yourself 'what if I could do *anything*?' Often people ask each other 'what would you do if you won the lottery?' People who have won millions in lotteries may surprise you in their choices. After playing with the money for a year or two, buying houses, holidays, and cars, they tend to get bored and look for something to do. Now that money is not the reason for working, they want something with purpose. This might mean investing in a business or starting a charitable foundation, or it might be taking up a simple trade. One lottery winner went back to his job as a staff trainer for McDonald's restaurants. So, if you win the lottery, what will you do two years down the line when you're bored?

Exercise 11.1 – Purposeful work

Stage 1: Remembering

- What sectors are suggested by the jobs you imagined doing in your childhood? (see Chapter 10)
- What are the most enjoyable subjects you've studied? How might they relate to work ideas?
- What work you have undertaken felt purposeful. Why?
- What jobs are done by friends or family that you find fascinating.
- What jobs have you seen advertised in the past which attracted you (even if you never applied for them). What was attractive about them?

Stage 2: Three great days at work

- Think about a time when you had a great day at work. The sort of day where everything went well and you went home energised. Write down what you were doing, what you enjoyed and what you achieved.
- Do the same thing for another two memorable days.

Stage 3: Imagining

- What jobs have you ever imagined doing?
- If you could try someone else's job for a day, what would it be?
- If you could do any job in the world for a week and still receive your normal salary, which jobs would you try?
- Who are your role models or champions, and what sectors are they in?

Stage 4: Trying ideas on

- What jobs have you tried, even for a few hours or days?
- What job on your CV was the most stimulating?
- What would you like to try next?
- Who could you interview or work shadow to find out more?

Career change: just do it

Reimagining career possibilities is engaging and useful, but when you discover something, they key question is: *what are you going to do about it?* The second half of this book is about finding exciting work, so let's be clear on one thing – if you want to avoid career change permanently, then carry on reflecting, analysing, and ruminating – that will surely prevent change from happening. So to prevent yourself saying down the line, 'I wish I had . . .', do something – and soon, especially if you have a sense that some new kind of work will feel more authentic, purposeful, more *you*.

Deciding what or who?

As discussed in the previous chapter, young people are often faced with dilemmas regarding job titles. It's often more useful to look at the mix of things we enjoy doing in work, and how far these activities fit the kind of people we believe ourselves to be. For many, not just those with a spiritual view of life, the important thing is *who* we are, not what we do. If this sounds like indulgent self-examination, look again at your career drivers and values to see how important these aspects are in work.

A good way into the question 'what kind of work would suit me best?' is to look at the overlap between what you are, what you do, and what you know.

Three Career Circles

Knowing

Chapter 8 revealed how preferred areas of knowledge provide powerful clues about meaningful work. Think about *what you have chosen to know about*. What topics, interests, and ideas matter most to you? One way of choosing a new sector is to think about the topics you like to talk and hear about at work. Review your areas of expertise, especially the underpinning knowledge you may be talking about in competency-based interviews (see Chapter 16).

Understanding the knowledge angle of work is also an insight into your motivation, both now and in the future, because it treats each job as a learning curve. Most roles are interesting in their first few weeks or months, but whether a job is intrinsically interesting in the long run is often about how much you will continue to learn and grow.

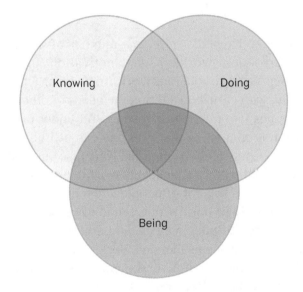

Doing

The phrase 'we are what we repeatedly do' seems to have been misattributed to Aristotle, but it's a strong idea. What we do shapes us, particularly those actions we repeat every day. You can turn this around to understand something equally important: *what we choose to do most of the time matters.* The activities that take up most of our waking hours have a strong influence on our effectiveness, work outcomes, and the way people see us. Remember that word 'occupation'? A job is something that 'occupies' our time and attention.

Skills (see Chapter 7) are what we repeatedly do. They move us towards outcomes, they shape our reputation, and they are important reinforcers of self-esteem. If you enjoy learning, your skills will need to be refreshed and updated; more importantly, they need to be used. Using only part of your skill set, or using skills you don't care about, can lead to long-term demotivation and cynicism.

Being

How you exercise skills reflects a number of things about who you are – your working style, motivation, and the values you express through your work. To perform a task well, accurately, with care, considering the needs of other people, and to be positive-minded or resourceful under pressure – these are not only signs that you have an attitude to work which keeps you feeling engaged, but also an indication that you've found work that seems worth your attention.

'Being' matters to a lot of people when they are choosing a career path. We're born with a range of personality traits, but we acquire attitudes, values, and ethics as we progress through life. What seems like dull work to one person can be satisfying and meaningful to someone else. Consider the kinds of work that allow you to 'be yourself', or work that feels more like a 'calling' (see below) than employment. Look at what your work does – does it improve the world, make someone's else life better, build or create something worth sharing? When it comes to work, *being* and *purpose* are intertwined.

What's calling you?

Do you sense that you might be looking for a *vocation* rather than just than a job? The word comes from the Latin *vocare*, 'to call'. It's used most frequently in terms of a life of faith, but even in popular usage a 'vocation' feels different from an occupation. Not only have we redefined what we mean by 'career' in the past 50 years, we have redefined what we mean by 'vocation', too. Some feel a 'calling' towards working with animals, being a chef, creating fine art photographs, making handmade furniture, or serving in the armed forces. Perhaps what these paths have in common is the love workers express for tasks, materials, or context – or their close connection with the people they serve, support, or inspire. A cabinet maker loves the wood, the tools, and responds to an urge to make something beautiful.

When we feel 'called' to the work we do, this provides a sense of commitment that is stronger than ordinary levels of motivation, and a sense of 'rightness' in our choice. It's not just a career impulse, not just this year's big idea. To choose a vocation often means turning your back on conventional career satisfiers such as money and status, and it is a pathway that may take years to explore and resolve. As Magdalen Smith (2019) writes, 'Vocation is often an unknown journey which involves humility as well as courage'. Many vocations require a commitment of decades, some a whole life.

Whether it's about doing something with great care or serving needs, vocations make an important contribution to society. A vocation may draw on particular gifts, or awaken abilities you didn't know you had. Other callings are simple acts of dedication.

You may assume that following a calling means forgetting about work satisfaction: the work is about duty, not about personal choice. This is an unhelpful assumption. A vocation may provide a strong sense of purpose, and will involve some sacrifice. However, living out a vocation can also be a good experience and is often deeply fulfilling. 'Good experience' isn't the same as 'fun', but shouldn't be a million miles from it. If you are called to some form of work, it should enliven you, at least some of the time. However, there are many glum-looking people in teaching, nursing, church ministry, and charity jobs. Living a vocation may be useful to society, but if it makes you miserable, you may be performing the wrong role in the right cause.

Perfection is as dangerous here as anywhere else in career choice. Those living out vocations will admit that they are not 100% committed to their calling all of the time. The difference is they keep to the path, trying to be authentic to that original calling, and to live out long-term life choices even when things are difficult.

Feeling called to a particular role can provide a strong sense of 'right fit' – you've found the place which is authentically *you*. Rowan Williams (1995) wrote: 'vocation is . . . what's left when all the games have stopped'. Your calling may draw you towards the best version of yourself. If you're uncertain if you feel called, there's another important consideration. A decision to follow this kind of path often arises from faith, strongly held personal values, or a sense of service. Perhaps the biggest feature of a calling is this: *it's not just about you.*

Here are three tests that might help if you're considering a vocation rather than a job. In a vocation:

1. The role feels right for you and others can see it's a good match for your gifts.
2. You commit to a long game, which may include fallow years.
3. You offer something which helps, feeds, or inspires other people. A vocation is a life lived for others.

Even if you don't feel you have a calling in the big sense of the word, remember that what you learn about managing your career can be enormously helpful to others. Share what's worked, and warn others of bear traps and dead ends to avoid. If you find what you're looking for, pass it on.

Exercise 11.2 – Getting your story in focus

As you become focused on what you want to do next, you need a short story capturing how your career brings you to this point.

Make notes in the right-hand column about what you will say.

Summary phrase – this might be a generic job title (e.g. *communications professional*) or a short phrase	I am . . . /Essentially what I do is . . .

Relevant background – a brief reference to your background	I started in . . .

Key strengths – relevant to where you want to go next. Talk briefly about skills, knowledge, or working style	What I enjoy doing . . .

What attracts me to this kind of role – short statements matching a few parts of your background to a sector or role	I find this kind of role exciting because . . .

Plans for experiment – things you'd like to start, develop, or complete in the role	I'd like an opportunity to . . .

Impact – what results you'd hope to achieve in the first six months	I'd like to achieve . . .
People outcomes (you might talk about this rather than impact)	I'd like to make people feel . . .

One client's story looked like this: **Summary phrase:** *I write stories about financial markets for institutions, general consumers, and private investors* . . . **Relevant background:** *I started in consumer research but became really interested in writing influential journalism* . . . **Key strengths:** *I really enjoy talking to market leaders and media contacts and understanding the key issues* . . . **What attracts me to this kind of role:** *The challenge of providing different messages for different audiences* . . . **Plans for experiment:** *I'd really like the opportunity to take corporate bulletins and annual reports online and make them more interactive* . . . **Impact:** *I want to get much more out of media contacts* . . . **People outcomes:** *I want people to feel that investment isn't a mystery* . . .

As you come closer to deciding what you are looking for, you will continue to ask questions but you'll also be asked to talk about yourself and say what you're looking for. This is a great opportunity to get across a short, focused version of your career story. Exercise 11.2 is designed to give you a positive, clear, memorable answer which helps people to recommend you. This is a story which explains quickly why you fit the kinds of role you now have firmly in your sights. Note how this structure moves quickly from past to present and makes tangible connections between your experience and the impact you will have in a role.

Career Change Test

Careershifters have designed a Career Change Test exclusively for readers of *How To Get A Job You Love*.

This short, free assessment gives you a personalised report designed to help you feel clearer and more confident in your shift.

You'll learn:

- Which of the five 'Career Change Stages' you're at
- How far you have the necessary foundations in place to make a successful shift
- Your most effective next steps – including pointers to which parts of this book are most relevant to you

Take your test at:

www.careershifters.org/htg-test

Careershifters helps bright, motivated people who feel stuck in the wrong career find and move into more fulfilling work. They do this through workshops, courses, free resources and a community that spans the world.

'Must do' list

Knowing	1. Review what you enjoy knowing about in the **House of Knowledge** (p. 100). 2. Review your preferred **work themes** (p. 69). 3. Use the exercises in Chapter 10 to translate ideas into **sectors for investigation**.
Doing	4. Review your **skills** and achievements using Chapter 7. 5. Use the **JLA Skill Cards** to identify your motivated skills (see p. 98).
Being	6. List your top three **career hot buttons** (p. 77). 7. Review your **personality** and complete the **values** exercises in Chapter 9. 8. Explore **purposeful work** in Exercise 11.1.
Master Sheet	9. Transfer the results of key exercises in this book to the **Master Sheet** (Appendix 1, p. 261). 10. Try the **Careershifters Career Change Test** – see link above.
Action steps	11. Show your results to friends and colleagues. Ask for ideas. 12. Tell people what you think you might be looking for – work on **Exercise 11.2 – Getting your story in focus**. 13. Look for conversations to help you find out more about interesting roles, sectors, and organisations.

12

The background to smarter job searching

'Attempt the end, and never stand to doubt;
Nothing's so hard but search will find it out'.
Robert Herrick

This chapter helps you to:

- Avoid the high/low game
- Make the most of your confidence window
- Interrogate job market myths
- Build productive relationships with recruitment consultants
- Discover the hidden job market.

Before you begin reading this chapter, be aware that Chapters 12–16 cover job hunting in depth – because knowing how to find a job is as important as knowing what you're looking for. If deadlines are tight, read Chapter 15 for a 4-hour job search programme, or Chapter 16 for interview tips. However, if you really want to take a little time to gain a bigger understanding of how to job search in today's market, read on.

The high/low game

Career changers of all generations, but especially market entrants, operate in high/low mode. For example, graduates apply to high-profile employers, forgetting that these organisations are swamped with applications. Having failed to get onto the shortlist for one or two 'five-star' jobs, they aim lower – much lower. They apply for low-profile, less interesting, no-star roles – because they look easier to get. They apply for jobs which could be done by someone with far less experience or qualifications. They begin to talk themselves into taking whatever comes along.

In today's market, this can mean taking a role that adds little to your CV and gives you problems in years to come. You're unlikely to get shortlisted for attractive roles in well-known organisations, especially if you apply cold without knowing what buttons to press. But if you can't persuade doors to open for five-star opportunities, dig deeper to find out how you can get closer to four-star roles.

Your confidence window

When you're looking for a new role, time matters. Researching opportunities and persuading people to meet you takes time, and organisations can take their time moving towards job offers.

Time matters for another reason – confidence. In general, people are optimistic as they begin a job search, and happy to try new strategies. As they encounter the reality of the job market, this confidence can easily fade. Many job hunters seem to have a confidence 'window' – a period of time when their confidence is high and then starts to diminish.

Confidence window

Many people go to the market too quickly, pitching themselves at jobs they don't understand with an unconvincing CV (see Chapter 15 on rookie mistakes). Not only is this largely unproductive, it impacts on confidence. They feel positive at first, but start to hit brick walls – sometimes rejection

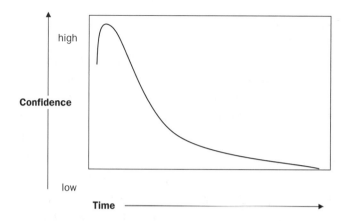

messages, often just silence. They start tinkering with their CVs (without knowing what to change) and begin to feel less confident. This means they become less adventurous in their job search strategy, and less effective at interview.

It's easy to see how confidence can be dampened. You apply for jobs online and don't receive any kind of response. You arrange a meeting with a recruitment agency but are told they can't place you. Friends and family tell you to 'take what you can get' (remember those limiting voices in Chapter 2?). You start to feel that you don't have what employers want. You network a little, but do it badly, and decide it's a waste of time. Your interview performance starts to go off the boil. You're tempted to apply for any role you see.

The good news is that confidence can be reinforced at every stage. If your job hunting isn't working, press 'pause'. Get some help to work out what you can do better. Reach out using online tools if you can't get in front of people. If you've only just started looking for a job, reflect on how you normally respond to rejection. You could copy the way writers proudly collect rejection slips, turning the process into a game. Or plan to spend time with supportive friends when you experience 'no'.

Job market myths

Let's debunk some classic myths. First myth: **'it's easiest to do everything online'**. As Chapter 13 will reveal, the internet is not a magic tool. It's great for researching organisations and opening doors, but applying online is a slow and frustrating process.

'Apply for as many jobs as you can'. Playing the job search lottery has one major consequence you haven't factored in – *disappointment*. Applying for roles where you're a poor match wastes an employer's time and sets you up for repeated failure. How much time do you think a busy manager will give to a speculative CV with no obvious connection to the company's needs? Every rejection, or zero response, knocks you back. Protect your resilience – make well-researched applications for roles where you're a credible candidate. Speculative approaches can give you access to the hidden job market, but only if they are well targeted and followed up by personal contact.

'Focus on advertised jobs'. This chapter outlines the way jobs have become invisible in the growing, and complex, hidden job market. Those roles which are advertised attract hundreds of applications, making it hard for you to stick out from the crowd. In addition, someone may be the preferred candidate before the advertisement is published.

'It's better to look for a job when you have one already'. Employers are highly influenced by recent experience and the ability to bring skills online quickly, so your most recent work history helps. However, organisations restructure all the time and many candidates are 'between jobs'. If you've been out of a role for a while, provide evidence of how you've kept your skills up to date.

'Qualifications are vital'. In fact, employers often have a vague sense of how qualifications translate into employable skills. Show how your skill set meets the needs of the job. If you are less qualified than your peers, emphasise what your work experience has taught you.

'You'll only get interviewed if you match the job description exactly'. Organisations sometimes want specific experience, but they often over-specify the job and rarely get someone who can do 100% of what's asked. Some employers are interested in potential, or expertise acquired in other sectors. Three things may get you into an interview if you are a career shifter: enthusiastic interest in the sector, real knowledge of the job, and the ability to show how your skills and experience can add value, even if your experience doesn't obviously match.

'You'll have to retrain'. Another powerful myth – believing that you will have to put life on hold and borrow money to retrain if you want to change career. Unless you are moving into something highly specialised with prescribed entry qualifications, you can probably enter a new sector and then pick up key skills and experience as you go along. Mistrust absolutes: if you're told that certain qualifications are vital, seek people who have discovered backdoor routes.

'You need to get out there and *sell* yourself'. How many times have you heard that? Over-selling can easily make you sound inauthentic, or desperate. Don't try to fake it or present yourself as a superhero. Simply present the best version of yourself, with clear supporting evidence. Listen more than you speak – focus on asking great questions. Discover how to talk about yourself authentically; it's easier to talk about things that interest you than to list your skills.

This links to another myth: **'you have to be a pushy networker'**. Networking works for everyone as long as they do it openly, honestly, and in a style that feels natural. Don't feel you have to dominate conversations and talk about yourself all the time. Learn to ask great questions and describe what energises you. Build relationships of trust rather than trying to exploit people (see Chapter 14, and my book *The Success Code*).

There are a host of other job-hunting myths to stop you in your tracks: '**A job's a job**', '**Think of the money**', '**Good jobs are hard to find**'. Okay, red card. Go back to Chapter 1. Do not pass Go. Do not collect £200.

How employers prefer to find new staff

Here's some information that in itself probably justifies the cover price of this book.

UK government research statistics show the way employers fill vacancies. Some methods are paid for – using employment agencies, for example, or paid-for job advertisements. Other, 'internal' channels cost little or nothing – job postings on the organisations' own websites or social media pages, for example. However, one free 'internal' method stands out in terms of popularity: word of mouth or personal recommendation.

An *Employer Perspectives Survey* commissioned by the UK's Department for Education was published in 2017. The report consulted 18,000 employers across the UK to find out how they recruited staff. According to the report, 81% of employers used 'multiple methods of recruitment'. 'External' resources often involved cost – for example, published vacancies, job boards, and staffing agencies. Some external resources were free, such as Jobcentres and university careers services. Employers drew on 'internal' resources extensively, such as an employer's own website or social media channels. However, the most important 'internal' resources used are almost entirely free of charge: personal recommendations and word of mouth.

Comparison with earlier surveys suggests that employers are increasingly using such channels. In total, 79% of employers surveyed used word of mouth or personal recommendation; nearly three in ten employers *only* used this method. Smaller establishments and new businesses tend to rely heavily on this approach. Some sectors (notably construction, 85% of employers) use word of mouth almost exclusively. It's clear that personal connections play an important role in recruitment, and informal, often personal recommendations are becoming increasingly important.

Employer safety habits

Building on what we know about employer recruitment methods, it's clear that employers and job seekers use totally opposite strategies, and see risk very differently. We will look at each employer strategy in detail below.

Staff are found through personal connections

Organisations like the security of hiring people whose work performance can be predicted, so they like to hire people they already know. If they can't find talent internally, they seek others close by. Some candidates feel this is about personal connections, but the simple fact is that organisations prefer people they know something about to complete strangers.

Employers act on word-of-mouth recommendations

If an employer doesn't already know someone, they don't rush to the market. They ask around. It's all about visibility. You might be recommended through a networking contact (or someone you met at an information interview). You may be known because you've worked with the organisation before. You might be visible because several people in a sector have mentioned your name.

Look around you. Who admires what you do and would be happy to recommend you to others? Have you enlisted help from these people as career coaches, dummy inter-viewers, idea factories?

How employers and candidates see risk differently

Perceived risk level for candidates	Employer method of attracting candidates to a vacancy	Perceived risk level for employers
High	1. Personal connections 2. Word-of-mouth recommendations	Low
Medium	3. Using external recruiters 4. Finding people using social media 5. Unsolicited approaches from candidates	Medium
Low	6. Advertising the job on the company website 7. Advertising the job externally	High

External recruiters

Sometimes organisations work closely with recruitment consultancies. These are important intermediaries standing between you and employers with jobs to fill. They can also become gatekeepers, deciding who to put forward. The vital thing is not to confuse them with career coaches; their role is to fill the job, not help you work through indecision. Working with external recruiters has positive and negative aspects for job hunters (see later in this chapter).

Social media

If an organisation can't find the right person through personal networks, it often reaches out via social media. Sometimes recruiters will approach you directly because your LinkedIn profile lists relevant skills or organisation names. At other times social media can alert you to the fact that an organisation is interested in meeting the right people.

Word of mouth happens in ways that are difficult to track. A friend may see a Tweet and mention it over coffee. You might reach out via LinkedIn and make a speculative phone call, or go through a formal recruitment process. Informal and formal, electronic and human – all becomes blurred. However, an employer is really asking, 'who do we know who knows someone worth talking to?'

How do you become a known quantity like this? Shine. Get to be good at your job and let others know it. Write articles or circulate good ideas. Keep an updated record of your achievements.

Unsolicited approaches from candidates

Unsolicited (speculative) applications can get a bad press from candidates who email hundreds of untailored CVs on a 'spray and pray' basis. Most will be ignored immediately. However, if you offer something credible and look employable, a door may open. They are interested to hear from candidates who can match future plans. Speculative approaches need to be highly targeted, matching organisational needs, and work best if you make a personal approach rather than relying on a cold email. Where an employer has let it be known informally that a vacancy exists, direct expressions of interest are usually welcomed.

Organisational websites and social media pages

Any organisation putting a vacancy on its own website is speaking to multiple audiences – current staff, those following the organisation online, and people well-connected enough to be directed towards roles through tip-offs and recommendations. Apply with careful attention to detail, matching your evidence against each job requirement. Research the role through your wider network.

External recruitment advertising

By the time an organisation decides to advertise a role, employer risk increases. The floodgates will now open. Job advertisements are often *candidate magnets* – all kinds of people apply, including many who are unsuitable. Many applications look undifferentiated – 'vanilla'. Your chances of being shortlisted are low, even if your skills are excellent, and yet many people put most of their time into chasing advertised roles. It's fairly passive: you fill in a form or submit a CV and then pat yourself on the back for a good day's work.

Someone relatively junior may be shortlisting, probably into three piles: 'No', 'Possible', and 'Yes'. In a competitive market, the 'Possible' tray is dispensed with. Work hard to get that initial 'Yes'. In your covering letter, use half a dozen bullet points to show you're a good match. Remember that reading a CV is a dull chore for HR professionals, and a frustrating distraction for line managers. Make your CV count (see *Knockout CV*, and also Appendix 2 in this book).

Working more productively with recruitment consultants

Recruitment consultancies find candidates to fill jobs for employers. Agencies range from high-street operations to executive search consultancies ('headhunters'). Although recruitment consultants keep candidate databases, they are largely vacancy-driven. They are most interested if you fit a vacancy that needs filling immediately.

Recruitment consultants have a major advantage: they have leverage to persuade an employer to see candidates – and issue job offers – quickly. Aim to establish contact with about 12–15 agencies that frequently fill the kinds of roles you are seeking. You will also be asked to register, sometimes online, but recruiters are people-oriented, so establish a relationship. This works best by meeting face-to-face. Find the names of individual consultants handling the roles you're interested in. Send a speculative email with your CV. Phone a couple of days later and ask for the opportunity to meet the consultant. Recruitment consultants like to be valued for their industry knowledge, and often agree to meet if they feel they can learn something about the organisations you've worked in.

Recruitment consultants have a good feel for the market and can provide sound feedback about how employers will react to your CV. Less professional agencies will flatter you when you register and never come back to you. Some don't know as much as they should about a job, and some will be reluctant to put you forward if you haven't done a similar role in the past.

A professional recruitment consultant will also tell you what you are worth in the marketplace, and what hurdles you will have to jump if you want to change sector. Many recruitment consultants have strong views about CV construction. Don't ask, 'what do you think of my CV?'. Ask instead, *'what does my CV say to you?'* Listen to the story coming back at you. If you recognise and like what you hear, your CV is working well enough.

Working with executive recruiters

The following are no-nonsense tips from an executive recruiter on how you establish and build good relationships with recruitment consultancies.

1. Focus on being exceptionally good at your job and making a positive impact. Good headhunters will then find you – but make yourself visible to them so that they can. Writing articles, speaking at conferences, and receiving industry awards all help.
2. Identify recruiters who specialise in your industry/ function and build a relationship before you're in job search mode by using your network to gain introductions and being helpful and considered when you're asked for recommendations; then prioritise who you want to stay in touch with. Don't forget you are divulging confidential information about yourself and potentially your employer, so do your homework around the recruitment company's reputation, expertise, values, and ethics. Do they feel a good match?
3. Strategically target the consultant within a firm who specialises in your function or sector. This individual

should facilitate connections to colleagues who might be pertinent to you – but you may need to ask them, particularly if you are open to changing sectors. Recruiters have a habit of putting you in a box, so it's better if you choose the box (or boxes) you want to be in. It is not necessary to contact multiple individuals within the same firm.

4. In terms of cold-calling a headhunter, email is still preferable to a phone call as a first introduction due to the heavy volumes headhunters receive, since it gives a quick impression of you and allows the headhunter to circulate your credentials among their colleagues and enter them into their global databases. The headhunter will immediately look for what is unusual or uniquely differentiating in your CV, so it's important you include quantitative information such as the size of the jobs you have held, organisations for which you have worked, the number of people you have managed, and results/profits for which you have been accountable.

5. The email accompanying your CV should give a quick snapshot of your career drivers: title, geography, compensation, and the types of opportunities you are interested in. If you do send a cut-and-paste email to a variety of headhunters, make sure it's personalised and all the typeface is in the same size and font!

6. Avoid 'spamming' headhunters with multiple unsolicited emails each week or phoning them several times in a day, as these efforts may backfire.

7. Be transparent without being overly self-promotional during any phone or in-person meeting with a representative from a search firm. Do not make claims that will not stand up to rigorous background and reference checking – the headhunter's duty of care to their

clients necessitates a reasonably thorough investigation of candidates, and they will quickly discover anything that is fabricated or exaggerated.

8. Assess opportunities proffered by headhunters realistically. Do not feign interest in a job that you are not intending to follow through on simply to get face-time with a recruiter – it will waste their time and not position you as a serious candidate.

9. When meeting the recruitment consultant, always have in the back of your mind that first impressions count: be prepared, be punctual, be smart, don't be afraid to 'use' the headhunter – ask for honest feedback on interview performance.

10. Once you've had a positive meeting or telephone call, ask the headhunter for their preferred method of staying in touch – phone or email – and how often.

11. Demonstrate that you 'know how the system works' by offering to help with open assignments; enhance your reputation with the headhunter by referring friends and colleagues that you hold in high regard (assuming they're at the right level and in a relevant sector) to them.

12. Be open with the headhunter about which firms you are trying to establish a relationship with – ask if there is anyone they would personally recommend. Share openly and honestly how the rest of your job search is going.

Joëlle Warren, Executive Chair, Warren Partners

The hidden job market

Having looked at employer recruitment methods and preferences, you may be coming to a conclusion: chasing conventionally advertised jobs, particularly on job boards, may not always be the best use of your time and energy.

A substantial proportion of jobs are not advertised. This is the hidden job market. Recently, I was criticised by a seasoned recruiter for continuing to refer to this idea, but the reality is that many job hunters have only a sketchy idea of how the twenty-first century job market operates. Most know that the hidden market exists; few know how to break into it.

If you want to slow down your job search *and* limit your options, do one thing: limit your job search to advertised positions. You'll miss out on most newly created jobs, all positions filled by word of mouth, and most jobs in start-up or small businesses. You'll miss out on all those companies that are just on the edge of thinking about creating a new job. You'll avoid opportunities where you are recommended.

We've seen how employers are increasingly relying on word of mouth to find talent. This trend looks set to continue – employers are keen to harness a range of free and cost-effective methods, including social media, so frequently fall back on the question, 'who do we know?'

We've looked at employer preferences. Any attempt to research the channels which work best for job seekers is problematic; in an age of instant communication, channels overlap. We know that some people get roles through existing or new personal connections – usually by knowing someone in the organisation. We also know from evidence that men find this method of job searching easier than women. Sometimes, personal connections happen by chance or instinct; at other times, candidates sharpen their interpersonal skills to get in front of people who can extend connections.

International studies point to a *rule of thirds* – on average about a third of all jobs are filled by word of mouth. The employer research discussed earlier in this chapter suggests that this proportion may be increasing. Similarly, about a third of job seekers find jobs using word of mouth. However, this data relates to *all* jobs, from shop floor level upwards. When you look at highly skilled, managerial or professional roles, or jobs in niche sectors, the percentage of those who find work through personal connections increases. In some sectors, senior roles are never advertised.

There are as many urban myths about the unadvertised market as there are job sites. The hidden job market seems confusing, largely because so much goes on under the radar. Communication channels blur and overlap. People hear about organisations that are interested in talking to candidates – through conversations over coffee, Twitter, news feeds, from other candidates.

What's running through your head right now? *You're going to tell me the answer is networking.* Well, in a way – your way. Find out more about organised discovery in Chapter 14.

'Open' may still be 'hidden'

If you think the fair way of finding a job is to throw your hat in the ring alongside everyone else, be warned. 'Unhidden' jobs may not be as 'open' as they look. Someone may have been promised it informally. There may be an internal candidate who everyone (apart from you) knows is in line for the job. Advertised positions can also have a hidden flavour: known candidates are told that a job is about to be advertised and warmly encouraged to apply – so they are automatically shortlisted. This happens more often than you think, even in the public sector. Employers sometimes have a preferred candidate in mind but go to the market to find benchmarks for comparison.

Jobs are filled every day without the market having any sense that a vacancy ever existed. This feature of the marketplace can take a lot of stress out of job hunting. If you meet an organisation and they like you, a job may be created around you. If an employer finds you through a recommendation, you can easily find yourself in a shortlist of one. It's all about being spotted, and becoming a known quantity.

'Must do' list

- ✓ Avoid trashing your goals early simply because things don't work at first.
- ✓ Spend more time and energy on the activities that shorten your job search and protect your confidence levels.
- ✓ Base your job search on reality, not job market myths.
- ✓ Take account of employer risk aversion in your job search strategy.
- ✓ Plan to approach recruitment consultants when your career goals and matching evidence are clear.
- ✓ Increase the chances of personal recommendation by telling people what you're looking for.
- ✓ Start your networking today – think of two positive-minded friends you can approach for encouragement and ideas. Reach out online if you can't easily meet in person.
- ✓ Check out Chapter 15 if you need results fast.

13

Hunting and connecting online

'Live in fragments no longer. Only connect . . .'
E.M. Forster

This chapter looks at:

- Why you need an online presence
- How to use social media as part of an active networking plan
- The classic errors people make online
- Online job searching.

Why the internet may not save your career

In the twenty-first century, job seekers make the same mistakes career changers made in the 1980s and 1990s. We're still essentially passive, waiting for the right opportunity to come along, waiting for the phone to ring, waiting for someone else to take control of our career. Before mobile phones, job hunters stayed home in case the phone rang. Now we sit at our desks and pray to St Google.

A large proportion of job seekers focus most on one activity: searching online. Why do so many people believe this is the quickest and best way to find a job? First, it's easy – job sites are readily accessible from hand-held devices. Second, sitting in front of a screen uploading your CV to job boards *feels* productive. Even more importantly, it *looks like work*.

Many job hunters believe the most effective method for finding a job is searching on the internet. There are many others. Being recommended by an existing employee is a highly effective job search method; many argue that this results in improvements in candidate quality, productivity, and retention. Word-of-mouth recruitment is also obviously cheaper for employers. Therefore, getting to know people in target organisations matters.

Some years ago, I helped out at a job workshop in the San Francisco Bay area. It was salutary to see that even in a relatively buoyant, hi-tech economy there were career changers expressing the same worries as job hunters everywhere. Local outplacement specialists had a rule: *Use your PC outside working hours. During the day, use shoe leather.* The web is fantastic for research, reasonably good at firming up connections, but poor at opening doors for the first time. A Tweet is forgotten in seconds, an email in minutes, a phone call in about half an hour. However, a warm face-to-face meeting (followed up by a thank you note) can easily be remembered for over 12 months. So, don't get locked into electronic correspondence – turn initial approaches into direct (private, offline) messages and then actual conversations.

Face-to-face meetings remain the gold standard. Since 2020 we have of course all learned to 'meet' online. The world of video discussions is not new, but we are learning to use it differently and more expertly, and the technology is rapidly catching up with need. If we travel less, more information interviews (see Chapter 14) will be conducted via screens.

Use job boards as a back-up system, not the main event

Job boards are useful, but it's tempting to rely on them too much. They are best used as part of a multi-strategy approach. Register with job boards that (a) handle enough traffic so that jobs relevant to you come up every week, or (b) specialise in sectors that interest you. Upload a good-quality electronic CV, and make sure you use key words that hirers are searching for. Be aware how applicant tracking software (ATS) is being used to screen applications. Research the key words that recruiters search for using the tracking software; include these words in any text that describes you, including online profiles.

Use job boards unconventionally, too. Use them to identify hiring organisations, and recruitment consultancies working for them. You can search by specialism, sector, role title, or by location to find organisations on your doorstep. Job postings reveal job titles as well as the language employers are using to describe top performers and key skills.

Don't ignore company websites, where you will come across jobs not advertised elsewhere. Large employers often invest a great deal in creating sophisticated career pages on their sites because they want to have direct contact with candidates.

Misunderstanding online job hunting

Job seekers often rely too much on the internet to find a new position: posting their CVs onto large CV banks in the hope that a recruiter will find them; searching online for job openings day in, day out; submitting untailored applications and then wondering why they never get a response.

I recommend limiting the time you spend online and having a clear four-step strategy:

1. Research companies to create a selective target list of suitable employers.

2. Set up relevant job alerts on aggregate job boards such as indeed.co.uk and glassdoor.co.uk, as well as industry-specific niche job boards.
3. Use social media to nurture and grow connections, raise visibility and credibility with recruiters and hiring managers (see material on LinkedIn below).
4. Follow companies and individuals, share their posts (if relevant to your networks), and contribute to the conversation with quality comments. Do this well, and you will get on their radar in the best possible way. Recruiters can search amongst candidates who follow the companies they are recruiting for, and regard such followers as 'warm contacts', as they have already expressed their interest in an employer, provided they are suitable candidates. Do the same wherever your industry, target employers and recruiters congregate – on social media or other sites (ranging from GitHub to Mumsnet).

Ruth Winden, social media strategist and career coach (careersenhanced.com)

How using social media can give you an edge

While some are happy to follow and update Twitter all day, others fail to see the point, or just see an embarrassing oversupply of trivial information. There are two main reasons you may discover that social media can make a difference.

The first reason is about *visibility*. How are people going to find you? When your name comes up in conversation, hirers look you up on social media. Will they find you online?

Does your online profile make sense to a target employer? Visibility leads to *recommendation*. When someone looks at your profile, which parts of it will encourage someone to recommend you? This is more important today because of the ever-increasing popularity of employee referrals, where staff are incentivised for introducing candidates to a business.

The second reason is *people*. Making a big life change is about relationships: making connections with people who will provide you with ideas, information, referrals – and encouragement. Your relationship needs to be with people, not with Google, but the best way to find and contact the right people now is to join (or even create) online networks.

Ignoring these readily accessible, free resources slows down progress, closes doors, and firmly suggests you have no interest in modern communication tools.

Using social media to underpin your job search

It's no use hoping someone will find you online by chance. You need a shop window that is easy to find and clearly sets out what you do. LinkedIn is an ideal tool for this purpose, as it's widely used, easy to manage, and gives you a great deal of freedom about how you present information. LinkedIn now offers three facilities: short updates, longer form content like a blog piece, and video. The last two are really helpful because they allow different ways of showcasing your interest and your evidence. A personal blog can be useful since it's one of the few online spaces where you have total control over content.

Look at your online profile with a critical eye. Is your main focus of work clear, at a glance? Are you including key words in your headline, summary, and work experience sections, so interested parties will find you? Are you supporting your professional achievements with facts and evidence? Evidence might include videos of presentations, blog posts, articles you were quoted in, photos, certifications, and any proof of your professional accomplishments. With diminishing trust in online information, it is more important than ever to back up what you claim.

Get someone to look at your online information. Ask them to summarise what they see. LinkedIn users have two ways of getting strapline messages across. The first is a job title (or a summary phrase that captures your role or expertise). This is very important, as it's usually taken as an indication of what you want to do next. Does this opening information put you into a useful box? Second, a 'status bar', a quick update on what you're doing. This is a great spot for featuring a topic or issue that you're focused on right now, or things you're investigating.

LinkedIn is for business, not letting your hair down. If you want to look like a serious, committed candidate, don't fill online space with updates on your cat or love life. Use a separate, friends-only Facebook account for that. If you live on the wild side, make sure that your on-screen confessions, conversations, and photographs are visible only to trusted friends. Many employers and recruiters use the internet for background checking. If you insist on posting photographs of yourself in a state of undress or inebriation, you might as well bring them with you to the job interview – it's called *public domain* for a reason.

Look for people, not jobs

If you want to change career by moving into a new sector, then focus on the one activity that is likely to make the biggest difference: *contact with other people.* You'll often hear the suggestion, 'It's not what you know, it's *who* you know, and who knows you'. However, as Chapter 14 will reveal, this idea is often used as a great excuse not to find anyone to get to know. The great advantage of social media is that you can make more contacts at greater speed than any previous generation. Contact details update themselves without you needing to keep records, and you can also follow people without being directly connected to them.

Although your ultimate aim is to get face-to-face meetings, you have to find some means of initial contact. Fortunately, most of the people you need to reach can be contacted online. An email out of the blue is likely to be ignored, so how do you use electronic communication to reach decision-makers?

Focus on an organisation that interests you. Look for named individuals – decision-makers with real needs. Follow their blog and Twitter accounts; find out what interests them. Be helpful – answer questions and share useful postings. Being genuinely interested in other professionals and their projects will get you noticed and can be a great way to start a conversation, develop a relationship based on common interests, and eventually open doors. Meaningful relationships take time to develop, so don't wait until you are job searching to build them.

Once you know something about a decision-maker, consider a direct approach. Ask yourself: 'Is there any approach method available to me other than a cold email?' Ask around: who do you know who works in your target organisation, or has worked there in some capacity, including a consultant or supplier? Referral from an existing employee will always get you in the door quickest. Use LinkedIn to spot people who are connected to someone in or near your target organisation. If you find someone you know who has a connection, pick up the phone and ask for an introduction. If that really isn't possible, make your own direct approach by email. When you do so, remember the principles of any job search letter: keep it short and focused, and spell out just two or three reasons why that person might want to see you. You're after a face-to-face meeting at this stage, not a job offer.

How to manage your online presence if you are between jobs

People are often unsure what to say online if they are unemployed. Don't use LinkedIn to broadcast the fact that you are out of work. Hirers and recruiters use LinkedIn to find experience, not availability. Don't waste the opportunities it presents by using your status bar to say that you are seeking work or still unemployed. Avoid statements such as 'have been looking for some time now' or 'will consider anything'. You wouldn't put that in a CV, so don't make it part of your LinkedIn profile.

Quirky phrases like 'looking for next great opportunity!' or the rather twee 'in the enviable position of being available to assist a new employer' sound like mild desperation. Your message is your expertise, not your empty diary. A phrase such as 'Qualified procurement specialist' is great – condensing experience and credibility into three words. You may, however, get away with a clear, focused, and unemotional statement, such as 'seeking full-time employment as an HR Manager in the East Midlands area'. Questions of tone are difficult to get right – ask the opinion of someone you trust to give you objective advice *before* you publish any statement of this kind.

Keep things updated: leaving your LinkedIn page dormant for several months signals a loss of interest; people assume you've found a position. Signal to recruiters you are open for job opportunities using the various tabs and options in LinkedIn, where you can define the type of employer you're looking for and also identify your skills. This information is relatively confidential as it is only accessible to recruiters, but needs refreshing regularly.

It's sometimes hard to think of updates when your only message is, 'I'm still here and still looking'. Refresh your status bar with updates on the things you are researching, and the things you want to know more about.

Think about ways of keeping your message varied and interesting. Make sure your online profile reveals activity, showing you're doing something for yourself rather than waiting for the market to come to you. Demonstrate enthusiasm, for example: 'Reading everything I can get my hands on about healthcare reform . . .', or 'Just watching a fascinating presentation on green building construction'. Show not just your interest, but the fact that you are up to date. Put in live links to websites, blogs, videos, and podcasts so that readers can learn more about the things that have inspired you. Bookmark interesting pages so you can send out recommendations on a drip-feed basis – one a day, for example, rather than a whole burst in one evening.

Since recruiters often find candidates this way, it's a good idea to include your email address on LinkedIn. Recruiters are always working against the clock and will often work with the candidates they can reach quickest.

LinkedIn: Top tips for job searchers

1. Think of your LinkedIn profile as a next step towards intimacy with someone who has just read your formal CV – consistent but more informative so that a reader can feel they know you a little better or more personally from considering it.
2. If LinkedIn is a high street, then your profile is like an individual shop from which you are selling expertise and experience services under your personal

brand. Use your first name and surname as simply as possible and in the same format as on your CV, business card, email address and signatures. Variations confuse.

3. Promote your business pitch succinctly next to your name and make it as unique as possible. Mine currently reads 'Careers Expert + LinkedIn Marketer + International Connector + Talent Catalyst + Start-Up Advisor' and at the time of writing is the only one out of 660 million users in more than 200 countries and territories listed on LinkedIn, compared to over 748,000 people who describe themselves simply as 'Career Coach'.

4. Upload a pleasant, friendly, approachable, smart, and professional looking photo of yourself. Colour or black and white is fine but do not use holiday snaps, arty poses, cartoons, symbols, company logos, or avatars. Choose who can see this picture.

5. Edit the URL that LinkedIn allocates to you so that it mirrors your name and personal brand. Then copy this detail on your business card, email signature, and CV to encourage people to visit your profile.

6. The Summary section of your profile allows you to craft, test, and communicate a powerful elevator pitch – and consider stating your contact details up front in the first three lines. Use the Specialties sub-section to list areas of expertise and interest for search engines.

7. Write a brief, positively worded description of your responsibilities and achievements in each position along your career path and enhance these with strong recommendations.

8. Join and follow alumni groups for everywhere you have studied or worked, as well as the largest and

most relevant LinkedIn groups in every industry or professional sector that you wish to explore. Monitor these daily for jobs and influential contacts, and actively participate in group discussions to connect or feed your expertise.

9. Link the Update box to your Twitter account and use it regularly to share your views, opinions, inspirational quotes, or authoritative articles sourced for relevance from your LinkedIn home page or credible external sources. You can also promote your involvement or attendance at industry events here and, similarly, more and more people are using this facility to upload photos or short punchy videos. Create content as well as sharing others'.

10. Frequency of decent quality content is the name of the game and done well, regular updates can make you look expert and raise your profile. By the same token, be mindful and careful not to look silly by posting inaccurately, clumsily, inappropriately – or too often. Incidentally, you can refine what you yourself see and make it more relevant any time by clicking on the 'three dots' symbol to the top right of every posting visible in your feed.

11. If actively job-hunting, maybe make it clear to recruiters that you are open to opportunities by activating the box and settings beneath your contact details on your profile page. But be very careful of doing this if you are already employed and do not want bosses to know you are restless or looking because this may backfire badly where you currently work.

12. Identify people you would like to connect with and personalise your template invitation message to introduce and contextualise your interest. If you don't already know them, perhaps start by

following their activity for a few days and comment intelligently in the discussion threads under their posts to get onto their radar and seed your later approach.

13. Research target companies via the search bar, then 'Follow' for news and contacts in those you want to target. Similarly, join the largest relevant special interest 'Groups' and participate tactically in their discussions, as well as monitoring for vacancies posted there.

14. Using the search bar, enter an ideal job title and company to identify relevant vacancies. Then see if you already have – or could readily create – connections inside the target business to chat with before you apply. This could trigger a personal referral that effectively puts you ahead of any lesser known candidates being considered for the job.

15. Use the search bar to reveal people with your ideal job title, organisation, and location. Their profiles will indicate how they got there and also identify any friends in common. Ask your mutual acquaintance to introduce you, then arrange an informational interview perhaps using the REVEAL method outlined in this book. This can be brilliant for establishing useful allies inside target organisations and win you fast access to the elusive hidden/unadvertised job market.

16. The 'LinkedIn Help Forum' can answer most questions about LinkedIn and typing 'use LinkedIn to . . .' on Google or YouTube will show you many more tricks too.

Julian Childs, career coach and business advisor (www.linkedin.com/in/julianchilds)

Can you get a job in 280 characters?

To use Twitter for job searching, set up an account specially for the purpose – you can make an impact with just a few followers. Twitter competes with Instagram, SnapChat, and Pinterest, but it's an important job search tool. Some great job sites broadcast through Twitter. Also, many key decision-makers use it as a platform for their thinking. This provides big hints about organisational culture – executives are likely to be more conversational and less guarded on Twitter than in other outlets.

Before you follow anyone on Twitter, it's important that you have a completed profile that shows, at a glance, who you are. This means a very short biography that includes useful and relevant hashtags, a summary of your expertise, your approximate location, and a link to a site that recruiters can go to for more information (a blog or your LinkedIn profile).

Present a succinct, understandable picture of who you are and what you do: keep it clear and simple. Don't overlook the simplicity of Tweeting clear messages, such as 'just got laid off, looking for a #job in #HR', because that may be enough to attract offers. Be consistent in your use of Twitter – become known for what you say and what you use the platform for, and stick to it.

Top tips for using Twitter when #job hunting

For earlier editions of this book, Matthias Feist set himself the challenge of summing up his advice in 11 tweets, using the hashtag #HTGAJYL, reprinted below. His tips work on the assumption that you know basic twitter functions and terms such as 'hashtag', 'mention', and 'retweet/RT'. Over the last two years, Twitter has changed – foremost in the doubled character limit imposed on users. This has led to more complex conversations being enabled. With it came the emergence of threads, multi-part tweets which act as microblog posts, allowing an author to address issues in more detail. Those threads sometimes span dozens of entries with multiple replies to each individual post. In this tradition, here is Matthias' thread. There are many tutorials available on the net. Find and share . . .

Thread:

1/11 tweets on using Twitter as a tool for #howgetajobyoulove, in support of @JohnLeesCareers new edition of How To Get A Job You Love #HTGAJYL. It's not sponsored content, but I will be in the book. I like John and his advice is IMHO excellent.

2/11 Create a Twitter profile connected to your other socialmedia profiles. Use the same picture and mission statement throughout for consistency. Put your Twitter name on your CV. Disable any settings that automatically tweet – be selective. #HTGAJYL

3/11 Follow target #employers, their followers, #job tweets, relevant bloggers and experts in the field. Following others brings you followers. Make sure they are real and don't spout only promotional or fake content. Curate your followers, block bots. Be choosy. #HTGAJYL

4/11 Use #LinkedIn to update Twitter not more than once a day. Never push all updates via LinkedIn, only work and audience relevant ones. Choose your message of the day wisely – always ask – what's of most value to my audience? #HTGAJYL

5/11 Tweet a lot, say about 5 times daily to keep a flow. Some still use email alerts for #socialmedia sites – so don't flood them. Consider e.g. Hootsuite to manage multi-platform posts: E.g. five tweets, one to LinkedIn, some to your Facebook page. #HTGAJYL

6/11 Only tweet what you think is relevant to your audiences. Use #hashtags picked up in relevant discussions, e.g. #HTGAJYL. Twitter at its best is when you share funny and snappy. Relevant visuals show that you are fun to work with. But don't forget – it's not Instagram.

7/11 If something good is not worth retweeting, like it. People react well to likes, and they drive engagement to their tweets. Adding value to their #professional Twitter feed will be good PR for you and the people you follow. #HTGAJYL

8/11 Don't worry too much about your original content at first, focus on sharing and adding value to others. Your first own tweets will always suck a bit. Relax. Twitter is immediate and boring content will just flow away. Move on. Others will, too. #HTGAJYL

9/11 Find your own voice: Write like you're in a #job engaging with peers: talk about topics relevant to #employers in twitter chats. It is OK to sprinkle in your own, even political opinion. But never be rude or spread #fakenews. Never #mansplain. #HTGAJYL

10/11 The Offline world is still important: go #networking and try to meet the people you tweet. Also, live-tweet from events. Even better, post pics, use Periscope to live stream and share your own YouTube videos. Visuals beat text every time. #HTGAJYL

11/11 Check interviewers' tweets in advance, quote or refer to them if appropriate. They will check you in advance, you can do the same. Follow speakers, but don't be creepy. Never say anything you wouldn't in front of other people and to their faces. #HTGAJYL

@matthias_feist – Matthias Feist works in higher education employability, enterprise along the whole student life-cycle at Regent's University London, and he is the ex-Chair of PlaceNet, the Placements in Industry Network. He blogs at www.matthiasfeist.com

Think about who will be following you

To follow you, people need to find your profile on social media. People want to know they've found the right person, so make sure you include up-to-date information about your location, specialisms, and work history. Posting negative information will slow you down like a dead weight. When posting online, don't say anything negative about yourself, past employers or bosses, or any of the organisations or recruitment consultancies you've had contact with in your job search.

'To do' list: Checklist for making the most of electronic media

✓ **Share personal information carefully.** People connect with people they know and trust. Trust comes from common interests, but also from discretion about the way you broadcast and use relatively private information. On LinkedIn it's best to focus largely on your working life and professional interests. Updates could include images of you working or volunteering. Leave wise quotes, cute pet videos and jokes to less formal sites like Facebook or visual sites like Pinterest and Instagram.

✓ **Protect your personal information online.** To avoid online fraud, choose carefully what others can see. Check your privacy settings regularly. Decide whether you want separate personal and professional social media profiles. Do not share your home address, birthday, personal or family details.

✓ **Create a compelling LinkedIn profile.** It's hard to predict whether interested parties will see this or your CV first. Both documents require compelling content. Think carefully about the way LinkedIn labels you with your current job title. Near the start of your profile, summarise your main skills, experience, and areas of focus.

✓ **Make it easy for people to find you.** If you're hard to find online, you probably won't be found. Increase your chances of being approached for projects, networks, opportunities, and job openings. Use industry-specific keywords. If applicable, add in hashtags (#) in your biography, headlines, experience sections, and summaries. Find these key words from job descriptions, industry publications, and leaders' profiles in your sector.

✓ **Make it easy for people to reach out to you.** If a request or offer heads towards you, a rapid response is vital. Decide what access you are willing to give – email only? Landline or mobile? Recruiters will ignore you if you play hard to get. Use your name in the same form across all media platforms. Personalise URLs wherever possible, ideally with your name only.

✓ **Create a positive visual impression.** A photograph makes your profile page seem friendlier and also firmly suggests that your posting isn't a fake being used to trawl for information. Use a bright, sharp photograph where your face fills the frame. Look professional but also friendly and approachable.

- ✓ **Stand out from the crowd.** With millions of profiles online, it's easy to be ignored. Don't try to appeal to everyone – think about the audience you hope to influence. Posts with images or videos get more attention than plain text. Build a reputation for the type of information you share.
- ✓ **Create links from your CV.** Enabling a hyperlink to your LinkedIn profile from your CV helps recruiters find more information about you quickly. If relevant to your target market, also add in your Twitter handle. Make sure CV information matches your social media profiles; job titles, dates, and employer names need to be consistent. Include additional evidence a CV cannot provide such as images or video, presentations (via Slideshare), or links to articles you've written or influenced.
- ✓ **Become a content producer or curator.** People seek you out because of what you know and who you're connected to. By creating, sharing, or curating information that serves your community of likeminded people, you highlight your focus – and attract relevant opportunities. Write a blog about a topic close to your heart; review books, products, or events; recommend people and organisations. Be selective and strategic about what you share. Contribute intelligently and in an informed way to key discussions. Keep abreast of sector developments.
- ✓ **Make better use of the internet as a research tool.** By scrutinising job ads and organisation websites, you can obtain detailed information about roles and what employers value in new hires. Keep

an eye on news items, press releases, and blogs from senior executives. Follow key industry figures, trade associations, and professional bodies.

✓ **Check inputs and outputs.** Visibility needs to be maintained, and you need to know quickly if someone is trying to reach you. Have a plan for maintaining the quality and quantity of your online contributions. Keep on top of your inbox: check email and voice-mail at least twice a day.

✓ **Make connections.** The more people you build an online relationship with, the more opportunities will open up. Online tools can connect you with people and opportunities well beyond your in-person net-works – so use them wisely. When you ask someone to connect on LinkedIn, personalise your invitation every time and give a great reason (rather than a bland 'I found you on the internet'). As soon as you are connected, continue the conversation, and aim to take it offline as soon as it feels comfortable to make a phone call or meet in person.

14

Organised discovery: how people will move you forward

'It requires a very unusual mind to undertake
the analysis of the obvious'.
A.N. Whitehead

The difficulty of doing the obvious

Chapter 12 investigated the hidden job market, showing how it has grown and how job searching has become more complicated.

I usually ask a new coaching client which job search method they think is most likely to bag them a job offer. Even at this stage most clients sense they will probably get quicker results through conversations and by making new connections. However, they are reluctant to do anything that looks like networking.

Nearly all job searchers, whether graduates or executives, hate that word: *networking*. They say it feels 'grubby', 'pushy', or 'it exploits people and loses you friends'. Some are even more honest: 'it makes me look desperate'. We should respect these suspicions. Anyone who suggests you start networking without addressing these issues is trying to get you to buy a jacket that doesn't fit, isn't your colour, and is something you'll never wear after you take it home.

I've talked about initial conversations with clients. At the end of a programme I ask: 'If you find yourself on the job market again, what will you do differently next time?' The answer is nearly always, 'I would start talking to people earlier'. Not 'networking', you notice, but simply 'talking to people'.

There are lots of reasons for talking to people. When an exciting opportunity comes out of the blue, this is rarely a random event. It happens because of the way you have managed your visibility. People have approached you because they know something about you. This doesn't happen immediately; first you need other kinds of conversations.

Networking for softies

Networking has acquired a tarnished reputation. You might imagine uncomfortable breakfast meetings where you're supposed to 'work the room', dishing out business cards. For most people, this kind of activity is as unproductive as it is dispiriting.

Don't call it networking. Reframe the idea: 'talking to people'. If you find this daunting, be assured that you can do this in your own style. You don't have to deliver a glib 'elevator pitch' – you'll get results by listening and asking great questions (for ways quieter people can make an impact, see my book *The Success Code.*)

Call it *meeting interesting people* – a way of putting yourself in the path of interesting ideas and organisations. Think of it as a way of following your curiosity, getting answers to questions. Connecting with new people is something we do all the time. If you move to a new town and want to find a good childminder, dentist, or plumber, you ask around. This is networking at its simplest.

Don't think of it as exploiting others. Networking should never be about trashing friendships for the sake of a job offer. Networks are *social* networks – they work best when we take a genuine interest in others. Be prepared to offer insights and information you've discovered. The process is about giving as much as taking – what has been described as a 'chain of helpfulness' or '101 cappuccinos'. Often you will form lasting relationships of trust.

Think of it as *building a community of interest*. Communities are not dependent on the total number of people they contain, but the connections between them. If four people are connected, that's 12 relationships. If you simply add one more person to the group, you get 20 relationships. As your personal web goes beyond ten, the number of possible interactions explodes. This shows the difference between mailing lists and interest groups. A mailing list may be 2,000 separate, unconnected people. An interest group as small as 2,000 can overturn national policy.

Be kind to yourself, and network like a true softie. Start with some practice runs. Take a friend out for coffee and say, 'this may come out all wrong, but can I try this out with you?' Ask anything you like, but *ask more than you tell*. Practise asking questions – about the work people do, how they got into it, what overlaps exist between their world and yours. Thank contacts for their time, but don't say goodbye until you've asked the number one, all-time, breakthrough networking question:

'Who else should I be talking to?'

Your two-breath message

No matter how many questions you ask, the conversation will always come round to you: 'What about you? . . . What are you looking for?' What you say next matters. On average, you take 15,000 breaths each day. With just two breaths you can say something that is short, memorable, simple, and upbeat:

> *'I'm interested in finding a job that allows me to do A and B and C . . . in an organisation that's doing X and Y and Z'.*

A, B, and C are your motivated skills – the things you do best (Chapter 7 helped you identify them). X, Y, and Z describe things your ideal employer is doing. You might mention specific kinds of products, services, technology, or approaches. You might talk about style (for example, hi-tech or cutting edge), culture (high quality or customer-focused), or the nature of the organisation (private, public, blue-chip, privately owned, etc.).

The two-breath message might remind you of the TV show *Ready Steady Cook*: you dump the ingredients in front of someone, then ask for a recipe to match. Responses typically include: 'That's interesting . . . Have you thought about . . . You really should talk to'. It's great when people offer sector ideas from your raw material.

Practise your two-breath message so that it flows easily and feels authentic. Listeners will respond well – it's succinct, unusual, memorable, and energised. It prompts much better responses asking for help identifying vacancies. You are dropping key pieces of information that people will remember and repeat, ensuring that the right messages come up next time your name is mentioned. (You can find a more developed version of messaging in Exercise 11.2 – Getting your story in focus, p. 145).

Degrees of connection

Daniel J. Boorstin (1984) wrote, 'The greatest obstacle to discovery is not ignorance – it is the illusion of knowledge'. We think we are aware of the limits of what we know.

In 1990, a play by John Guare – *Six Degrees of Separation* – premiered in New York. It played with the idea that you can reach anyone in the world in a short chain of connections. Person A leads you to B, B to C, and so on. Even if you begin with someone with only the vaguest connection to your target, you can get there in six conversations – or less.

I regularly ask audiences, 'who's met someone who has been into space?' Twice in my life I came close to famous astronauts without even trying (Yuri Gagarin was Manchester's guest of honour when I was watching from my pram, and some 40 years later Neil Armstrong spoke at a venue 10 minutes' walk from my office). Even though the first manned space mission was Gagarin's flight in April 1961, only a few hundred people have been up there. Yet, in my average audience, around one person in 50 has talked to someone who has been in space. For some, these astronaut encounters are life-changing moments. Even the most extraordinary people are not that far away.

With large audiences I often finish by prompting everyone to ask someone sitting nearby one question: 'What are you looking for?' If there are 300 people in the room, about half a dozen will sneak out at this point, claiming an urgent appointment. This is sad – these 140-plus conversations will include some amazing moments. Later someone from the audience will find me and say, 'You know, I had a conversation today which may have changed my life'. The fact that it happens every time means *it just happens* – you just need to keep asking.

Information interviews

A job interview is about persuading someone to offer you a job. An *information* interview is very different. Information interviews are one of the easiest forms of networking. Its main purpose is to unearth information. Even though the technique has many benefits, it's used by a small minority of career changers.

Information interviews are most helpful if you plan to change sector. Why? Because your maps are blank – your Satnav brain thinks it's in the middle of a ploughed field. You don't know what you don't know. If you apply for roles, you'll be guessing at organisational needs. You need to know a lot more to become a credible candidate. Desk research will help, but you get there more quickly – and with many additional benefits – by talking to people. Start by finding someone who knows about a work sector, and ask them to meet you. Never ring anyone cold. Start with people you know well – *the people you can ring without having to pre-pare words in your head.*

This isn't about selling yourself. It's mostly not about you at all. You'll be finding out about someone's role, organisation, and sector. It's a low-stress process, because you're armed with a script (see below). It's not about telling, projecting, self-promotion – it's about absorbing information. This isn't pushy networking in disguise, and you're not subversively trying to obtain a job interview.

An information interview is a vital stepping stone to **discovery**. Conversations provide deep-level information – far more than you will ever glean from a website or company brochure. It's the inside story – what a job really feels like, and the realities of organisational culture. These interviews are also a key stage in improving your **visibility** – vital in the hidden job market (see Chapter 12).

Information interviews – why they are useful

☑ **INFORMATION BENEFITS OF INFORMATION INTERVIEWS**

- For a short but critical time, you put *research* before *job search*.

- You meet people in real jobs by moving from desk research to field research. You will learn about entry routes, sector trends, and organisational cultures.
- You understand the reality of jobs, so you can begin to decide if they will suit you.
- You spot the roles and sectors that match your skills and experience.
- You pick up clues that will help you match yourself to specific roles.
- You understand how top performers are described.
- You pick up the language you will need for job interviews.

☑ VISIBILITY BENEFITS OF INFORMATION INTERVIEWS

- People remember you, especially if you see them face-to-face and thank them in writing afterwards.
- People remember your energy, your enthusiasm, your commitment, your reason for enquiring.
- The people you meet make connections on your behalf. Your name is mentioned when problems and opportunities arise.
- You learn enough information to sound like a credible candidate really committed to moving into a new sector.
- You are often talking to decision-makers, putting yourself on their radar for when problems or opportunities arise.
- You plant carefully chosen information about you which is remembered.

☑ JOB-SEEKING BENEFITS OF INFORMATION INTERVIEWS

- You learn more about jobs using this method than by applying randomly for roles or asking to be told if a vacancy comes up.

- You identify target organisations.
- When people understand what you're looking for, they can help you. If you're remembered, opportunities find you.
- You pick up insider language that allows you to convince people you really understand the sectors and organisations you're targeting.
- If you broadcast employable skills and knowledge via social media, you may get direct approaches from recruitment consultants.
- Your visibility may put you straight onto a shortlist, even if a job isn't advertised.
- You discover jobs before they become vacancies.
- *You fall over jobs.* It's true. Ironically, the indirect route, which is not focused on job search, often turns out to be the number one strategy for getting at the hidden job market. The roles you discover might not be right for you – if so, pass them to others in your network.

☑ **CONFIDENCE BENEFITS OF INFORMATION INTERVIEWS**

- You get to wear smart business clothes and visit places of work, which maintains your confidence levels in a job search.
- You get used to asking great questions and conveying memorable energy.
- You get used to talking about yourself, briefly.
- If you're changing sectors, you learn how to make your experience and skills sound relevant.
- Since you're tracking down people who share your vision of what work is about, you'll end up with new social contacts and friends.
- You leave people with a positive impression of you, and enough information to recommend you to others.

Big and small asks

Information interviews work because they don't ask for too much. Think about how you react if someone rings you out of the blue and says, 'I'd appreciate your help in identifying jobs in your organisation'. You'd feel uncomfortable. You don't know the caller, so why would you recommend this person? The conversation would probably end there. Asking someone to look over your CV is a 'big ask' – it takes a lot of time to read a CV properly and then give useful feedback.

A request for an information interview should sound like a *small ask*. It should sound like someone can deliver what you need with minimum effort. Don't ask for career advice, or for a recommendation, or for tips on getting hired by the organisation. Just ask about the person in front of you – people often find it easy to talk about themselves and the job they do. If you make the conversation easy, people are usually prepared to pass you on to someone else.

The REVEAL method

REVEAL conversations are meetings with people who can talk in an informed way about the work they do. They add to your knowledge, expand your network, and reveal how jobs feel from the inside. A meeting won't bring you to a once-and-for-all career decision. It won't be a job interview – but sometimes will lead to one.

There are tough ways of persuading people to see you. You could try working through the Yellow Pages. You could turn up at reception and ask for a meeting. Either might work, but they present an uphill struggle. Begin with people you know – so you never have to make an awkward phone call.

Start with **three people**. You already know them well. They are easy to talk to. They might simply give you encouragement, information, or answers to some of your career questions. Start practising your REVEAL script. Ask how they got into their careers and what's happening in their work sectors. Ask, 'who should I talk to next?'

Can't think of anyone to talk to? Perhaps that's just your way of avoiding making a start. Even people who never think about networking usually have about 100 people within their immediate contact circle. If you're feeling a little more confident, reach out to people you're connected with through social media.

Ask for a soft handover

Practise with people you know reasonably well, build your technique, and then get introduced to new contacts. Getting introduced means you never have to make a cold call. *At the beginning of every conversation*, say something like this: 'I'm hoping to speak to about a dozen people in this sector to gather a wide range of views'. Later, when you get to the end of the conversation and say, 'That was really helpful. Who else should I be talking to?', your colleague will probably already have thought of a name. Or several. If face-to-face is tricky, ask for short discussions using Zoom or Skype.

If you're offered names, you've only done half the job. A list of phone numbers or email addresses means you're back to cold calling. You have no choice but to begin by saying, 'You don't know me . . .'. It takes confidence to get past that difficult moment, so avoid it. Ask for a *soft handover*: 'Do me a favour. I hate ringing people cold. Would you please phone ahead to say why I'd like a conversation?' One set-up phone call (or email) means that your next contact expects your call and knows what it's about. The soft handover reassures the next person along that you're not selling anything, not a time waster, and not after a 'big ask'. When your next meeting begins, often you only need mention the name of the last person. This should be a good enough prompt ('Sure – Jack called me about you'). Draw on personal connections between one contact and the next ('Sue tells me you're a keen fell walker . . .').

Ask for 11 minutes of the person's time. 'Five minutes' or '15 minutes' is too vague. You can conduct a REVEAL interview in 11 minutes. If you stay longer it's by invitation, because your conversation partner wants to know more about you.

Ask for a face-to-face meeting. You learn far more – about the person, the organisation, and its culture. It increases the chance of being remembered, and the chance of a long-term relationship. Face-to-face wins every time. Some contacts may try to get you to settle for a phone call, but be frank about the fact that you learn more by visiting people in their place of work. If the person is a long distance away, you may need to do what you can by phone or by email. Ask, 'who do you know in my part of the country . . .?'

It's a conversation

Now you've considered the benefits of information interviews and looked at the REVEAL script, reset your thinking by one notch. It's an interview, yes – because it has structure and purpose – but it shouldn't feel like one. Make it feel like a *conversation*. Don't ask too much, don't stay too long, and don't make contacts feel interrogated; if they enjoy the interaction, that encourages them to stay involved. Keep things relaxed, so it feels like an inquisitive and energetic exploration, a conversation between like-minded people rather than something stiff or transactional.

Conducting a REVEAL interview

You've got there – you're in the room with someone who can help you.

What on earth do you say? The REVEAL method offers you a simple, effective script. Use the suggested questions a few times until you get the hang of the process and develop your own phrasing.

REVEAL stages and key phrases	Notes
Recap *Key statement*: 'I'm here because . . .'	Recap how and why this meeting has come about. Remind the listener of who introduced you, and why the person in front of you has been recommended as a contact. Say what you hope to get out of the meeting. Mention that at the end of the conversation you'd be interested in referrals (e.g. 'I'm trying to talk to about a dozen people in this sector'). At the end of the interview, you can then ask for further contacts.
Explore *Key statement*: 'I'm here to find out as much as I can about . . .'	Your opening question emphasises that you have asked for a meeting to help your exploration. So, get started. Perhaps open with 'how did you get into this line of work?' Move on to more in-depth questions about the sector you're exploring, e.g. 'What do you find most interesting about this sector?' Move the focus onto hiring patterns – how people normally get into this line of work. Probe the conventional and unconventional ways of getting work in this sector. This part of the conversation is when you ask most questions.

Vision *Key question*: 'What have been the biggest changes in this sector recently?'	You're asking your contact to improve your vision – so you have a clearer understanding of the sector you're investigating and how it's changing. A good supplementary question is: 'What changes can you see coming along in the next year or two?' Answers will provide useful clues about additional research you might undertake, key players, and organisations you should be talking to.
Excellence *Key question*: 'What kind of people are doing well in this sector?'	Ask what top performers look like. This is far more effective than asking 'how do I get a job?' Answers will reveal the skills profile of successful candidates – useful information to store away for the first time you match yourself against a role competitively.
Action *Key question*: 'What should I do to find out more?'	By now you've learned a lot and you don't want to outstay your welcome. So, being business-like, you move to your next action: 'If you were in my shoes, where would you look next?' Draw your interview to its conclusion by seeking ideas for organisations and sub-sectors to research. Make a note of suggestions.
Links *Key statement*: 'Thanks very much for your time today. As I mentioned, I'm keen to talk to a number of people in this sector. Who should I be talking to?'	Show how much you have valued the conversation. Build on the suggested actions by focusing on names of people – links in the chain of connections you're going to build. Seek the names of two or three new contacts: '*Who else* should I be talking to? . . . Perhaps you can recommend a couple of other people who can give me an equally useful perspective?'

	If no names are forthcoming, probe for: • names of organisations • names of information brokers, for example, branch chairs of professional bodies • the names of helpful recruitment consultants specialising in this sector. Make sure you get a *soft handover*: 'I hate ringing people cold. It would be great if you could phone ahead and let your colleague know why I'd like to have a conversation . . .'

Follow-up

Too often people think the best, natural follow-up to a REVEAL interview is to send a CV. Wrong – remember, it's a big ask. If you want to send a follow-up, use an email to summarise your background, interests, and top skills – in no more than six bullet points. A short email is often acted upon immediately; a long or complicated request gets put to one side.

The simplest way of following up is to send an old-school 'thank you' card. Yes, a real card you send through the post. Buy a quality one with an attractive image on the front. Write inside it how the meeting was useful to you and what has happened as a result. Most people, if they remember at all, say 'thank you' by email. A card expresses gratitude with more care and attention, and that's appreciated. Quality cards are hard to throw away, and often remain on a notice board or under the glass of someone's desk for several months. Ensure your contact details are included somewhere discreetly on the card so it's easy to get back to you.

Don't send further requests for help unless you really need to. It's better if you send something helpful – an article, a link to a useful web page, a book recommendation, or an introduction to someone else.

What if I am invited to consider a job?

Don't let the meeting become a job interview – that's a breach of trust. If a specific position enters the discussion, say you'd like to go away and prepare for a proper interview. Offer a time when you are free within the next few days. Ask for full details of the job and prepare thoroughly, even if you are in a shortlist of one. That way you come back fully prepared, matching your strengths to the key requirements of the job.

Following the maze

It's easy to feel sceptical about information interviews. People naturally ask, 'how long does the process take?' and 'does it really work?' It's hard to predict in advance which conversation is going to get you the biggest result. It's like working your way through a maze. The treasure could be there at the first turn, around the next corner, or deep in the maze. You have to trust and keep searching. With persistence, there is magic and surprise in the process – the next conversation could just be helpfully informative, or it could change your life.

Things will happen along the way. You will meet people who will help you at future career turning points, and you will make new friends. You will have fascinating conversations and meet some very interesting people. Thank them for whatever they provide, even if it's just encouragement.

Three predictions

Prediction one: you already know at least one person who can really help. When we begin networking, we scan the far horizon for people we know only vaguely. Who do you know who is close by? There's a simple test: you're looking for the kind of person you could pick up the phone and talk to without having to plan what you're going to say.

Prediction two: whatever job search methods you use, *you'll probably find a job through someone you know already, or someone you meet in the next three months.* Play the game backwards. Who are you going to call for the first conversation?

Prediction three is about breakthroughs. Those who teach information interviewing at expert level often argue that the best results come from the third circle of networking. You start with people you already know, and they introduce you to second circle contacts, who you may know vaguely. Those contacts introduce you to an entirely new group – the third circle – composed of people you don't know at all. This third circle gives you the best feedback, because they see you objectively, and the most useful leads, because they project you into worlds you know nothing about.

Exercise 14.1 – Who can you reach?

Networking for softies means that you start with people you already know, but it's useful to have some sense of where you want your conversations to take you. Start with the questions you want answered. What sectors do you want to know about? What organisations would you like to reach? What jobs do you want to find out more about? Start with a list of questions and topics.

Against each of these topics and questions, write a name. Someone who works in a relevant sector. Someone who used to work in that sector. Someone who knows people in a wide range of occupations. If you get lots of names that's great, but you only need two or three to start the process.

It's possible to build up a personal web of between 60 and 100 useful, curious, and interesting people within about three months. Keep a note of the name and contact number of people you are trying to reach. Have the list to hand in case someone calls you. Set a diary reminder of follow-up actions agreed.

Exercise 14.2 – The Connections Game

As you investigate sectors and ask great questions, names of organisations will come up. Your personal research will add new names. Work towards a list of target organisations. You might eventually want to work for one of them, but at this stage you just want to find out more.

List them on a spreadsheet:

Organisation name	Contact person	Tel/Email	Score/10	Next step

Now play a game. In the 'Score' column give each organisation a score from 1 to 10. A score of 1 means you know nothing about the organisation apart from its name. A mid-range score means you know a lot about how the organisation operates, its style and culture, and the kind of roles they regularly fill. A score of 9 means you have at least two people inside the organisation, and 10 means you are close to at least one decision-maker capable of making you a job offer.

Your goal is to improve each score by at least one point every week. Column 5 records your planned next step. Reach out to people via LinkedIn or your personal network, and keep asking for warm handovers. This way you keep building connections and shaping what other people know about you.

'Must do' list: Ground rules for information interviews

- ✓ Use the REVEAL structure. Keep practising to build up your confidence.
- ✓ Don't stay too long unless it is at the other person's insistence. Don't ask to be shown round the building or site, but warmly accept the offer if it is made.
- ✓ Don't ask about specific job openings because that undermines everything you've said about the purpose of the meeting.
- ✓ How you operate reflects on the person making the introduction. Turn up on time, and don't ask for more than your contact can deliver.
- ✓ Be ready for the question 'and what about you?' Try out your two-breath message (see p. 187).
- ✓ Don't forget to ask for three names. It's very easy to go home missing one of the main reasons for the meeting.
- ✓ Get people to hand you on. Don't call cold unless you have to, and only do so when you're clear about what to say.
- ✓ Send a thank you card a week or so afterwards: it's an unexpected gesture, and you will be remembered.
- ✓ If you send a follow-up email, don't attach a CV, which is a conversation closer, but use bullet points as a reminder of what you're looking for.

The 4-hour Job Search Programme

'My thinking is first and last and always
for the sake of my doing'.
William James

This chapter helps you to:

- Avoid rookie mistakes
- Understand what will extend, or shorten, your job search
- Improve your market readiness
- Get tangible results in just 4 hours
- Develop a multi-channel job search strategy.

Your condensed 240-minute programme

This book is designed to take you through a process of change leading to a well-planned, multi-strand job search. Career coaching aims at getting you the right job at the right time. Early results matter (see the confidence window on p. 150).

You may want to begin job searching in a hurry. Be careful – it's easy to go to the market too soon, with the wrong message. You may spend a lot of time and energy doing things which are unproductive. You may put out misleading messages or influence key people in a way you later want to undo.

However, there may be reasons you want to make a quick start – financial pressures, for example, or an opportunity with a short shelf life.

What can you achieve in 4 hours? Perhaps more than you think. You can judge your own market readiness, and improve your evidence and key messages to the marketplace. You can quickly put your shop window in order, and learn strategies designed to shorten your job search. You can plan to get quick results using the right evidence, assisted by a balanced, effective job search strategy. You can make the most of technology to reach people who are not available for in-person meetings. And you can avoid rookie mistakes.

Why do smart people make rookie mistakes?

No matter what new electronic tools are available, we keep making the same basic mistakes when job searching. Even in a tight market, candidates submit indifferent CVs or fail to tailor them. Others talk themselves out of the job in the first minutes of an interview, or never understand what the organisation is looking for. As Chapter 1 outlined, looking for a job looks tedious and deceptively simple. Although there's clear evidence of what works – and what doesn't – even experienced candidates try to make it up as they go along.

Look at the classic mistakes people make in the first month of job searching. They pitch poorly constructed applications at high-profile roles in well-known organisations. They email out unfocused, untested CVs to all their contacts. They apply for jobs online and, because they receive no response, they rewrite their CVs or go for lower status roles.

Don't spend the first three months recovering from job-hunting mistakes you make in week one. Make the best of your early energy; use your time more effectively. Avoid throwing yourself at the job market with indifferent material and little sense of where you're going. Resist the temptation to make random, desperate-looking applications for jobs that mean nothing to you. Don't set yourself up to fail by putting yourself into situations where negative results are guaranteed – for example, applying without understanding organisational needs, or going to agencies with little idea about the roles you're seeking.

Activities likely to make your job hunt LONGER

These are things you might be doing right now which *extend* a job search:

- Relying solely on the internet to find jobs.
- Pursuing only advertised positions which puts you in competition with hundreds of other applicants.
- Applying for jobs you don't really want 'just for the experience' (and yet feeling flattened by rejection).
- Applying for exciting jobs at first and then 'lowering your sights' when things go wrong.
- Using up all your best contacts in the first three weeks and then complaining because you don't know anybody.
- Submitting a CV full of clichés, empty claims, and little solid evidence of achievement.
- Going to interviews with under-rehearsed answers.
- Networking without knowing why you're doing it or what you want to say.
- Spending too much time looking at screens, and not enough time with people – approaching potential contacts by email rather than by phone.
- Approaching your most senior contacts with a vague request for help and advice rather than specific requests.
- Chasing jobs in declining sectors (rather than seeking out the sectors and organisations that are experiencing growth).
- Applying for random jobs with random messages.

How closely does this list describe what you've been doing recently? Now we turn to activities which will give you a better return on time invested.

Activities likely to make your job hunt SHORTER

Here are methods for achieving positive results in the shortest timescale:

- Road-testing your CV before you send it to important contacts.
- Rehearsing what you want to say about yourself, especially before getting in front of important people.
- Using social media to research people and organisations, but also to make connections and build new relationships.
- Moving away from screens and towards telephone or video conversations and face-to-face meetings.
- Networking of any kind – even just talking to friends and neighbours about job ideas can make a difference.
- Conducting information interviews (see Chapter 14) so you get under the skin of target sectors and really understand what they are looking for.
- Using your best contacts at the right time – approaching senior people only when you're clear how they can help, and you can give them two or three reasons why they should recommend you.
- Telling everyone you know what you're looking for, keeping it focused and simple (see 'two-breath message' on p. 187).

Market readiness

Recruitment consultants talk about 'market readiness' – a state of preparedness that means you're ready to make the most of opportunities and you can safely be put in front of decision-makers. How do you know if you're market ready?

Exercise 15.1 – Market readiness

You'll know if you are market ready if you have answers to the following 5 basic questions:

Questions	Your answers
1. Why are you on the market right now? *Danger areas*: talking negatively about why you left your last job, or sounding desperate to get a new role.	
2. What are you? *Danger areas*: trying to cover too many options, or sending out conflicting messages about your main work role.	
3. What are you looking for? *Danger areas*: sounding like you lack confidence, or are hesitant about your next steps.	
4. What are you good at? *Danger areas*: not being prepared to talk concisely (but authentically) about your strengths, with examples ready for interview.	
5. What makes you stand out from other candidates? *Danger areas*: sounding over-confident but unclear about the demands of the job, or uncertain about what you have to offer.	

These questions might appear difficult and you might be saying 'I'm not ready' – however, they can be answered more quickly than you think.

Getting results in 240 minutes

To work through this book takes a day or two. Readers tell me they enjoy reflecting on their 'career DNA' but they also want short cuts to get results quickly. Reasons for time pressure vary. You may have an opportunity in your sights, or you might feel under pressure to 'get out there' and start applying for roles. There are results you can achieve in 4 hours. Here's a simple programme to help you do just that.

A 240-minute job search in 7 steps

Step 1 – Look at your launch platform

Are you set for blast off? Look again at the 'market readiness' questions above. When someone asks, 'Why are you on the market right now?', how much are you likely to reveal about disappointment and uncertainty? Decide now (with the help of others if necessary) whether you're ready to begin Step 2. (See also Chapter 18 for tips on job readiness for those leaving full-time education).

Plan how you will use your time. What job search strategies are you going to use? Half an hour's planning now will make a big difference. Work out how close you are to a working CV (this isn't just about cataloguing your experience, but matching your evidence to fit target roles).

Step 2 – Get active

One way to misinterpret this book is to think it's purely about self-examination. You need to look out as well as looking in. Don't allow yourself to believe you can only act when everything is ready – the perfect CV, the well-stocked contact book. Don't wait until you feel you can make flawless job applications. And don't wait until people have time to meet you face-to-face if you want a conversation quickly. It's important not to throw yourself into job hunting unthinkingly, but it's easy to delay. *Good enough* is fine, *perfect* gets in the way.

Begin to get active by reaching out to people who can remind you what you're good at: tapping into other people's knowledge; picking up the phone to contacts to find out more about work sectors. You can get stuck into an active search by spending just 45 minutes in online research and a couple of phone calls.

Step 3 – Get used to talking about yourself

Knowing something about your best self isn't enough – you need to get your evidence across. The key to fast-paced job hunting is in some ways very simple: knowing what your message is, and how to make it stick. Many job hunters are floored the first time someone asks, 'what skills do you bring to us?' or 'why should we consider you for this role?'.

Practise talking *about yourself* – particularly your areas of uncertainty – before sitting under the spotlight. This will make you more focused and less nervous in the first round of interviews. If you find talking about yourself difficult, remember that you will get better at this through *repetition* (tricking your brain into thinking this is routine, familiar territory rather than a minefield) and *technique* (practising what you will say and preparing for tough questions). Spend at least 30 minutes practising. Talk through your work history with a friend. How do you talk about the high points? How do you talk about your best skills without sounding egotistical or inauthentic?

Work out how to organise your material so you can get several key messages across quickly (see Exercise 11.2 – Getting your story in focus, p. 145). Learn how to communicate why you are on the market at the moment, but also your career story as a whole – if you don't make sense of your skills and experience, an employer won't. For sensitive issues, prepare your Safety Zone Responses (see Chapter 16).

Step 4 – Be clear what you're looking for

How do you achieve this kind of clarity? That's a fair question – much of this book is designed to help you explore a wide range of options. However, if you're in job search mode, saying 'I'm not really sure what I am looking for' tends to put the handbrake on.

Start dealing with the possible, not the unlikely. Use the two-breath message (see p. 187) while exploring, but for rapid results, start to focus that down even further. Name organisations, even if you are just using them as examples. Write down a target list of organisations you'd like to approach. Focus on actual job titles that might come up. Develop an action-focused target list (see Exercise 14.2 – The Connections Game, p. 201).

Use the list below to focus on the ingredients most likely to get you shortlisted.

Role clues to help if you want to be shortlisted quickly

- The role makes sense in terms of your background, skills, and knowledge.
- It makes sense as the next chapter in your CV.
- The first page of your CV contains at least half a dozen matched pieces of evidence to get you shortlisted.
- The job will stretch you, even if only marginally.
- You have at least 75% of the requirements of the job description.
- The organisation is keen to make an appointment soon, and you can contact a decision-maker.

Step 5 – Feature your best self

As you learn about work and jobs, organise information *about you*. Look elsewhere in this book to find methods of cataloguing your skills and know-how, and talking about your strengths, working style, and achievements. Take 30 minutes to organise your raw material so that you have the first 50 words of your CV or LinkedIn profile. Decide on your key messages for interview.

Your 'best self' isn't a fake version of you, but *you at your best*. What are you good at? (Use the relevant chapters in this book to check out your skills, working style, and to remind yourself what motivates you in work).

And now the killer question. What makes you stand out from other candidates? This obviously relates to specific roles and sectors, but spend at least 1 hour before every interview planning to pitch your best material. For each role, offer not only your best self, but your *best-matched self*. Focus on the top items an employer is seeking, aligning them with strong pieces of evidence from your history (see Chapter 16 on interviews).

Step 6 – Get ready to launch

Set out your stall. Make a list of projects you have completed during your career and measurable achievements you're proud of. Find supporting evidence to demonstrate skills and know-how. Catalogue your material and use the best of it as the main features in your CV.

Benchmark yourself against jobs. Use the internet to research the names of jobs you hope to chase, and the skills and qualities they're looking for. Match your evidence, especially in terms of skill level and the language you use to describe what you're good at.

Find someone with hiring experience to give your CV a 'cold read' (in other words, they don't already know your work history in detail and you don't explain your CV first). Ask the same person to grill you with questions based on your CV and jobs you're applying for. Practise your interview performance thoroughly before you go anywhere near a selection process.

Deal with problem goods in your shop window. Does your LinkedIn profile say what you are and summarise the key strengths you want the market to know about? (see Chapter 13). Look at any gaps in your CV – time gaps in terms of work history, but also credibility gaps in terms of your experience, your qualifications – prepare to explain why you should still be considered.

Market-test material as you develop it. Broadcast on all channels: use a multi-strategy job search (see below) to get yourself in front of decision-makers.

Step 7 – Search smart

To get quicker results, engage in multi-channel job searching. There are many channels which will take you closer to jobs – job boards, company websites, recruitment agencies, social media, direct approaches to organisations, headhunting, and word-of-mouth recruiting. Candidates often rely on just one or two channels, and many prefer to rely on online job boards. This is rather like deciding that whatever your health problem, your only remedy is aspirin. Don't ignore the online world – just give it the time it deserves.

Today's job market is complicated, with lots of distractions and dead ends. As Chapter 12 revealed, employers are shifting recruitment strategies. To succeed, you need to operate using all channels, not just the channels you prefer. Combining job search methods increases their power, and unlocks the hidden job market. What do you prioritise? Anything that gets you in the room with a decision-maker or closer to an organisation with an identifiable need. Spend your time and energy wisely; focus most on activities that shorten your job search and protect your confidence level.

'Must do' list: Multi-channel job searching

✓ Research work sectors, and build up a list of target organisations.

✓ Undertake temporary or project work that increases your visibility to decision-makers.

✓ Scrutinise job advertisements to identify likely employers and useful agencies.

✓ Monitor internal job boards operated by employers.

✓ Conduct information interviews (see Chapter 14) to deepen your understanding of sectors, while improving your contacts and visibility.

✓ Be visible and distinctive on social media. Use LinkedIn to reach out to informative and supportive new contacts (see Chapter 13).

✓ Follow up recommendations to talk to people and organisations, but do your homework first.

✓ Talk to people who are at the heart of great networks.

✓ Talk to recruitment consultants who regularly advertise jobs in your target sectors.

✓ Approach companies in your chosen sectors on a speculative basis. Write a cover letter matching four or five of your key areas of experience to the employer's needs.

✓ Submit carefully matched applications in response to interesting vacancies.

Getting better results at interview

'Take nothing on its looks; take everything on evidence.
There's no better rule'.
Charles Dickens

This chapter helps you to:

- Deal with interview anxiety
- Rethink interview preparation and performance
- Plan for tough questions
- Improve the way you get evidence across
- Negotiate a job offer.

For question-by-question preparation, turn to *Knockout Interview*. This chapter provides an overview of the worst of what an interview can put you through, and the best that you can draw out of yourself.

How we only pretend to prepare for an interview

Everyone takes interviews seriously, but not everybody prepares well. Professional interviewers regularly see candidates who have not planned for basic questions. They expect the interviewer to do the work, dragging evidence out of them, or they hope to 'wing it'. Why do otherwise savvy people leave so much to chance? Probably because interviews are stressful experiences we would rather not think about.

Interview nerves

Anxiety has a positive side to it – adrenalin sharpens the mind. It can also get in the way of what you say. Don't beat yourself up if you experience stage fright – a bone-dry mouth, or getting the shakes. You can't conquer interview nerves overnight, but you *can* take immediate steps to reduce their impact. For example, if nervousness makes you clumsy, don't accept a drink if it's offered, practise sitting still and talking about yourself calmly and clearly.

Nerves can also result in a blank mind – failing to remember great evidence from your CV. This is where preparation counts. Good planning means you won't hope to pull material out of the air, but you will match your evidence in advance, point by point. By analysing job documents, you will learn how to predict around 80% of interview questions – yes, four out of five. Most are big, obvious topics related to job content. Knowing that, you can no longer get away with saying, 'I've no idea what they'll ask me'. Planning to improvise means you plan to experience stress.

Exercise 16.1 – Employer shopping list

Obtain a job description for a role that interests you. Take an A4 piece of paper and divide it into two vertical columns. In the left-hand column write down, point by point, everything the employer is looking for.

List all the 'wanted' elements: qualifications, experience, know-how, etc. Some things on the list will be desirable, but note everything described as 'essential'.

In the right-hand column, write your matching evidence. Write down a phrase or a bullet point to match each point. Each will be an achievement or a bit of experience. Later you will turn these experiences into evidence by shaping them into stories. When you trawl for evidence, look again at Chapter 7 on skills and achievements.

Look hard at the employer shopping list. What skills and experience are listed first? What questions is the interviewer definitely going to ask?

Telling tales

Interview time is expensive for organisations. Where candidates talk for too long, this frustrates the process and makes it hard to cover all questions. It also risks losing the interviewer's attention. Compress your evidence into mininarratives. Your material becomes easier to remember, giving you confidence that good material is within easy reach. Also, you keep your listener's attention. We like stories, particularly if they are entertaining, attention-grabbing, or just interesting. We remember stories for much longer than we retain information, and we remember energised stories for longer still.

For every topic, shape your notes into a short story, with a clear beginning and ending. Make each story sound fresh (don't repeat phrases printed in your CV). Tell it as *your* story – interview clichés suggest you're just another nondescript candidate. Plan how each story will begin ('Let me give you an example of where I've done that . . .').

Half-prepared candidates just 'think about' answers. Fully prepared candidates have pre-packaged answers to tricky questions. Practise stories which last about 2 minutes. You don't have to learn each one word for word, but be clear how each story begins, and how it ends. Use a simple structure – for example, identify a problem, explain how you dealt with it, and talk about the final result.

Great stories add sparkle to your answers, drawing on the 'bottled' energy discussed in Chapter 4. Rehearse stories by speaking them out loud at least three times. Speak your lines in front of a mirror, checking that your body language tells the same story as your words.

Working in the right room

Interviews can look like hard work. *Avoid doing any work at all in the interview room.* This doesn't mean being laid back (although being a little more relaxed always helps). However, if you work hard at anticipating questions and practising stories, you'll have done all the work in your living room, not the interview room. Anticipate surface-level questions relating to the job description, and then dig deeper. Talk to people who know the organisation; find out how success is described. Now think: what demanding questions might you be asked, knowing your own shortcomings? Where do you need to sharpen up your evidence?

The human brain is troubled by the unfamiliar. Rehearsal and repetition trick your brain into thinking it has done something before so often it seems routine. Having pre-processed stories at your fingertips means you listen to interview questions more carefully and work harder at maintaining a positive relationship in the room. Practise talking about yourself – rehearse stories so they are concise and energised.

If time is really short, use a simple formula: **six plus three**. Match stories against the **six** items in the job description you think are most important, and then get **three** additional points across about why you're well matched to the role. This is especially useful in initial, screening interviews, which are a quick check that you match essential criteria.

Exercise 16.2 – The Politician's Trick

Listen to a senior politician being interviewed on the radio. No matter what questions are asked, the minister always manages to make three or four strong points about government policy. The questions just provide an opportunity: the airtime is being used as a way of getting a particular message across.

You can use the same technique:

- Step 1: Look at the key areas of a job, and ask yourself: 'What three points is it vital that I make during this interview?'
- Step 2: Write them down, and rehearse a clear, concise way of talking about them.
- Step 3: Communicate these three points at interview. Politicians know that their listeners can only hold a few ideas in mind at one time. Interviewers are much the same.

First moments

You're being assessed from the first time you are seen by the organisation. Reception staff are often asked for feedback. Dress one or two notches smarter than the normal dress code for the organisation. Leave your coat, bag, and umbrella with reception – it helps to create a picture that you already work there.

Opening interview moments are like a screen test. Do you look and sound like someone who fits the role? Present yourself as an energised, relaxed person who's easy to work with. Speak clearly, audibly, and at moderate speed, even if you're just talking about the traffic. Signal reassurance to the interviewer – you fit in, you can do the job, and hiring you won't look like an embarrassing mistake.

You don't have to 'fake it'. False confidence and fictional claims are evident to seasoned recruiters. Friends give you the advice 'just be yourself', but that doesn't help very much.

Better advice might be: 'show the interviewer what you are like on a good day – the best version of you that you can bring into the room'.

Top 10 interview tips

Given that most people know they need to turn up on time, look reasonably smart, and sound coherent, I've compiled my alternative 'Top 10' list:

1. Remember, **you're the guest not the host**. Allow the interviewer to play the role of host and enjoy the courtesy afforded to you as the guest. If you start to put the interviewer on the spot by saying, for example, 'What's your management style?', they won't enjoy the interview so much. Often candidates have played the role of interviewer more than interviewee and find it hard not to undermine the interviewer. The host needs security of control over the situation and the accolade of being trusted to be the interviewer. The guest needs to be comfortable and looked after – understand this is not a weak position.

2. **People buy from feelings** not from cognitive thoughts. People feel more intensely if you offer pictures not facts. Pitch your achievements through well-told stories – involve and engage the listener, allow them to empathise.

3. **Integrity and enthusiasm are the hardest qualities for any interviewer to resist**. Integrity means that when working with you, they will always know what's going on and can always trust you. You won't undermine their own position or cause them embarrassment. Enthusiasm shows confidence, generates

energy, and is infectious – they always love offering the role to the person who *really* wants it!

4. **Visualise a time you performed at your best** – play it in your head like a film reel repeatedly a few days before your interview to remind yourself of how brilliant you can be. Allow yourself to believe in your own propaganda. Then, at interview, perform from the part of you that performed so brilliantly in your 'film reel'.

5. **People watch for things to emulate** – observe and register aspects of other people's personality, performance, and appearance and decide which aspects feel right for you to take on board. Decide what the 'grown-up' version of yourself looks like, collecting ideas from colleagues to consciously create a more effective and powerful version of yourself.

6. **Perform from your work head not your home head**. Often people feel stripped of their title and brand when they lose their job. Be clear about your own brand – if you were an Operations Manager, you are still an Operations Manager and have the experience to prove it – your brand is your industry experience. If you go into an interview with your home head on, you are more likely to feel vulnerable, exposed, overwhelmed, and lack clarity of what you are offering. Go in with your work head – clear of your own brand and its appeal in the competitive marketplace.

7. **'What are your weaknesses?'** There is usually something in a job specification you lack or where you lack experience. You could just ignore it at interview, but when the interviewer compares you with other candidates, this hole in your credentials is bound to be discussed. It's better to talk openly about

the issue so you can put a positive spin on it and talk about how you plan to overcome this minor gap.

8. **It's not about giving a good performance but about giving the best performance**. You can pretty much guarantee that the company will have a good selection of strong candidates to interview with the requisite qualifications and experience, all of whom can pull off a decent interview. So, what's the point in being one of the crowd? It's not about taking part, it's about winning – there are no second prizes. Try to challenge yourself throughout the interview to consider not what's a good answer but what's the *best* answer. Ask yourself, 'what can I say that nobody else can? How can I put it in a picture so that they *feel* more intensely, and I become a compelling candidate?'

9. **Determine three things you'd like them to think about you in the first 90 seconds**, and use all your powers of non-verbal communication to portray those three things. Plan it into your appearance, manner, gait, and tone. It's amazing that so often people pick up what you're thinking without having to say a word. In fact, only a tiny part of the impression you make comes down to what you say – everything else is non-verbal.

10. **Don't try to 'close'** – this sales technique gives people the creeps and they can see right through it, making you a less attractive candidate. People on the whole don't like to be sold to. Show how much you want the role, and give clear and confident evidence of your achievements with enthusiasm and integrity. Remember that in the final stages of selection, you will have at least one other candidate in competition – you have potentially a 50% chance of

getting the offer. However well you felt you got on with the interviewer and however well you answered the questions, at this stage, you can guarantee your competition also felt the same! Keep up the job search right until you sign a contract.

Kate Howlett, managing consultant,
John Lees Associates

Improving your performance

How can you improve your interview skills? When asked for interview feedback, risk-averse HR departments generally say things which are bland and vague (you may get a little more if you ask about one way your interview technique could be improved).

You will get more useful feedback from practice interviews with colleagues who have some experience of conducting hiring interviews. Use real job descriptions and ask to be interviewed against them as well as your CV. Use the *exact* words you plan to use in a live interview rather than saying 'I'll probably talk about . . .'. At the end of the practice interview, ask for objective feedback about your impact, your evidence, and your body language.

Building relationships at a distance

The habits of social distancing enforced during the lockdown of 2020 meant that far less interviews took place face-to-face, and far more happened by video link (especially preliminary, screening interviews).

The principles remain the same – good stories, accurate focus on job requirements, and building a relationship with the interviewer. The last element is a little harder where technology gets in the way. Do everything you can to establish rapport, using small talk to make the conversation as human as possible. Be thoroughly prepared with all key documents in front of you, and make sure that you are uninterrupted. Remember that if you're talking to a screen you establish eye contact when you look at the camera, not at the person.

Preparing for off-the-shelf questions

Interviewers sometimes come up with novel questions, but usually ask job-focused, 'textbook' questions, including the following:

'Tell us about yourself'. This is a deceptively simple opening question. An employer wants to press on, so will be frustrated if your answer is lengthy. Don't unpack your entire work history. Offer a quick overview of the shape of your career and summarise your key skills.

'Why do you want this job?' Employers like to hear career stories that make sense. Don't apologise for your CV or suggest that it's a series of random events. Rehearse a quick summary of your career that shows how it is a single story with different themes that knit together, and then talk about how the job on offer is the perfect next step for you.

'Why are you changing career?' Give a clear reason why you plan to move into a new sector. Don't dwell on what has dissatisfied you about past roles – discuss positive reasons for change.

'What are you most proud of in your working life?' Practise talking about career high points which show you are motivated and can add value in a role. Prepare stories of times you rescued a situation, delighted a customer, or handled a difficult project.

'What motivates you?' Talk about what you have to offer rather than what you want to gain. Discuss the skills you enjoy using and what you hope to learn. Stress the benefits to the organisation. Show rather than tell – don't just say you are committed and energised – provide examples that prove you are.

'Tell me about your strengths and weaknesses'. Plan to talk about three or four strengths required by the job – with good examples ready to hand. If there are any gaps in experience, emphasise that you're a fast learner. Don't linger on weaknesses – name one skill you would like to develop.

'Are you a team player?' How easily do you fit into a team? Provide examples of what you've added to a team – or, even better, where you've encouraged a team to work more effectively.

'How quickly do you pick things up?' Employers want a quick return on recruitment costs, so they love fast learners, people who can hit the deck running with minimal supervision. Talk about a past job – or study experience – where you got on top of a difficult problem quickly, organised your own learning, and got results quicker than expected.

'How do you respond to pressure?' An employer wants to know how you respond in a busy workplace, and how calm you will be when things go wrong. Give examples of times when you have met difficult deadlines or handled tricky people, kept your cool, and got the right result.

See 'Safety zone responses' below for more advice on answering tough questions.

Show you're in charge of your career story

You need to show you can do the job, but also that *the job matches your career story*. Do you apologise because your

CV is 'all over the place' or because you 'jumped around a bit'? You have one career, and there are advantages to talking about it as one, coherent, story. When applying for a new role, talk about what you hope to learn from it, and how it fits as the natural next chapter in your career story.

If you have changed jobs frequently, talk positively about reasons for change, and what you learned at each stage. Interviewers respond well to phrases like 'I guess I was lucky because . . .' or 'that turned out well . . .'.

Talking about competencies

Competency questions require a special kind of preparation. Where competencies are listed, match them point-by-point in your application, and then prepare a mini-narrative to address each one. Set the scene briefly, outlining challenges or problems you faced; talk about what you did, and the outcome. Be prepared to say what you learned from the experience and what you might do differently next time.

Competency stories will usually feature a mix of skills, underpinning knowledge, working style, and your attitude to work. In some panel interviews you may get one shot at an answer, so be careful to cover every part of the named competency. Even with highly structured answers, tell engaging stories. Average candidates generalise ('What I usually do is . . .'). Strong candidates talk about specific events.

Safety zone responses

What questions do you hope the interviewer will forget to ask? Which probing questions do you dread? Prepare short, upbeat, uncomplicated answers which keep you firmly in your safety zone.

Be brief – this prevents you getting bogged down in a difficult topic. Staying upbeat reinforces the idea that you can overcome difficulties and stay in charge of your career story (see above). A simple structure moves from past to future. For example, dealing with redundancy: 'Like a lot of people I was laid off when the organisation restructured, but it's given me a chance to focus on what I really want to do ...'.

Work on these responses before you go anywhere near a decision-maker. If you're dealing with an especially difficult topic (for example, you dropped out of university), plan a second line of defence to anticipate probing questions.

Interview questions where safety zone responses help

'Why didn't you complete the course?' People drop out of learning programmes all the time, but it's often difficult to disguise the fact on a CV. Don't go into great detail about why a course didn't work for you. State simply that it wasn't giving you what you needed, and you made the decision to try something new.

'What did you like and dislike about your last job?' Likes – make a good match between the things that motivate you in work (for example, people, challenges, new learning) and the key things on offer in this new role. Dislikes – talk about things that frustrated your work performance such as bureaucracy or computer failure rather than talking about individuals.

'How do you respond to criticism?' Employers don't have time for ruffled feathers or workplace squabbles. Treat this question as if it is really asking about how you respond to feedback. Give examples of times when you have adjusted your working method or tried new approaches. Don't complain that the criticism was unjustified.

'Why are you on the market right now?' An employer wants to know whether you are moving on from choice or circumstances. If you were made redundant, mention this briefly, then talk about the work you want to do next. Avoid saying anything negative about a previous employer. If you've been unemployed for some time, emphasise your continuing learning and the range of organisations you have looked at. Don't complain about how difficult the market is, or how many rejections you've received. Employers will also probe reasons for job change, so rehearse short, positive stories covering these issues.

'How did you get on with your last manager?' Avoid criticism of past bosses. Everyone's working style is different, so show you don't let personality issues get in the way; give examples of where you have worked with a range of colleagues and bosses. Explain different strategies you have used to communicate with people you found difficult.

'What's been the biggest challenge in your career?' Prepare an example of something where you achieved success (or at least came out fighting). Negative information lingers in the mind of interviewers, so pick a positive story – ideally one that showcases skills that are useful to the hiring organisation.

'We've seen a lot of talented people. Why should we hire *you*?' You're unlikely to have one 'killer' feature that puts you ahead of the competition. Describe how your skills, know-how, and experience combine together in a unique way to make you the best person for the job. This is often a good opportunity to shake interviewer beliefs: 'You might assume that I don't have enough experience in this sector. In fact . . .'.

Your chance to ask questions

The final question is often 'Do you have any questions for us?' – too many candidates politely say, 'No, you've covered everything in great detail, thank you'. Wrong answer! Interviewers remember the first and last things said at interview more clearly than anything else. Your final questions are a great opportunity to leave a lasting impression.

Some interview guides try to persuade you that this moment is a great time for you to fish for information to help you decide if you want the job. This is wrong-headed. An interview is about securing a job offer. You can decide whether you want the job by research outside the interview room. Don't ask questions which suggest you have doubts. The purpose of your final questions is *message reinforcement*, not information gathering – a final positive impression signalling your interest in the role. Prepare three great questions (ask only two – have one spare in case a topic is addressed earlier in the interview).

Before you ask a question, say something positive about the role. Then your question sounds like your buying signal: you like the job so much you want to know more. Don't waste the interviewer's time by requesting basic information you should have learned from the company website. Ask questions that show familiarity with key result areas. Clarify how results will be measured, and probe outcomes to be achieved in the first six months. Ask questions about the future of the job: What changes are anticipated? How will the job adapt to those changes? What learning opportunities are on offer? These questions demonstrate enthusiasm, *and* help the interviewer imagine you doing the job. Once an interviewer sees that picture, it's hard to shake.

Interviews with recruitment consultants

Recruitment consultants are professional selectors who make a living finding workers to fill vacancies for client employers (see Chapter 12). They don't make the final selection decision, but are critically important gatekeepers who determine whether or not you get on to an interview shortlist. Their credibility depends on presenting well-prepared, credible candidates, so if there's something about your dress code or interview behaviour that raises questions, an experienced consultant will probably give you feedback. Sometimes they will grill you about your suitability for a role – useful preparation. Additionally, because the recruiter has looked at the role in detail, you can ask for tips on matching your evidence.

Rejection

In the average job search, you will be rejected more times than accepted. Even if you don't get the job, you can learn a huge amount about your perceived market value. It's trite to say that you shouldn't feel rejected if turned down by an employer. It may take a while to bounce back, and that's understandable. Do remember that candidates are rejected for all kinds of arbitrary reasons – sometimes simply because a large number of applications are received and only a few candidates can move to the next stage.

In any job search you will hear the word 'no' more frequently than 'yes'. This is a neutral statistic that has nothing to do with you. Even the best salespeople in the world know they need to hear the word 'no' at least three times before they get a 'yes'. The problem is that when the 'no' is to *you*, it can knock you off balance. Be careful not to use 'no' as junk evidence to support negative statements: 'I knew my background wasn't strong enough. . .'.

Talking money

At any stage in the process you may be asked what you want to be paid. The golden rule is to keep off the topic until the employer wants to offer you the job – the moment when you have maximum leverage. If the topic comes up earlier, you might mention a salary above or below an employer's expectations.

Base any pay level you request on hard knowledge of market conditions. Find out what pay range normally applies for the target role, and what evidence you should present to be in the top 10% of that range. Emphasise the value you will add and the size of the problems you will solve. Alternatively, saying 'I'm being interviewed for jobs paying between £xxx and £xxx' shows your market value impressively.

If possible, wait for an offer before naming your price. If the offer is too low, take some time to think about your next step. You might come back and ask for a better offer, or you might choose to renegotiate some other part of the job – see below.

'Must do' list: Questions to ask yourself before accepting a job offer

1. **Does this job add to my CV?** What will this job add to your career story? How will it help or hinder the way you present yourself to a recruiter in five years' time? Have you done this kind of job before? If so, what's new about it? What will you learn in this job?

2. **What parts of the offer do I want to negotiate?** Work out what matters to you most from the long list of things that candidates regularly include in the deal at this stage – money, flexible working, leave, relocation or travel packages, start date, location, pension, health benefits, car, even job content. The important thing to realise is that you can only ask for leverage on a maximum of one or two points, otherwise it sounds as if you are being difficult. Second, never try to renegotiate something you have previously agreed, as this is seen as unprofessional and can cause the whole deal to collapse.

3. **What's the team like?** Don't just ask, find out for yourself. While the formalities of a written offer are being completed, ask to spend a couple of hours with the team you will be joining. This confirms your strong interest in the job, but also helps you to be sure that you will fit in, and tells you a great deal about organisational culture. If the organisation turns down your request, you might wonder what's in store.

4. **Do I understand why I am being hired?** If you're unsure what the role is all about, you should certainly

be seeking more information before acceptance. Clarity about what's expected of you and what problems you're expected to solve can help enormously with the first 90 days of the job. It's also useful to know what they see in you – the reasons you've been hired are closely linked to what the organisation will see as success (see below).

5. **Should I try to influence role content?** This can also be a good time to negotiate what you will actually be doing in the job. You certainly won't have the same leverage for at least another 18 months or so of taking the job, so if you feel there is any possibility that you can tweak the job description so that it suits you better, try including this as part of the 'deal'.

6. **What does success look like?** Get a handle on the way you will be judged within four months of starting the role. Ask about preferred outcomes and what's expected of you, so you don't face unpleasant surprises down the line.

Exploring different ways of working

'The voyage of the best ship is a zigzag line of a hundred tacks'.
Ralph Waldo Emerson

This chapter looks at:

- Rebalancing and refreshing your career
- New choices in working arrangements
- Exploring portfolio careers
- Temporary, interim, and flexible working arrangements
- Working for yourself.

Changing the way you think of your career

Two generations back we enjoyed an unusually high degree of job security in return for company loyalty. Workers of the twenty-first century face a very different world. Jobs are created and lost at great speed as organisations restructure themselves frequently. A career no longer seems a simple path; it will probably be built of several strands and multiple experiences.

For around half a century management writers have been predicting a decline in permanent, full-time roles, and an increase in flexible working (interim, contract, flexi-hours) and self-employment. These changes haven't arrived as quickly as commentators have suggested. However, work is changing. Workers today are, for example, likely to find themselves in occupations that are not closely related to their initial qualifications. Even though everyone knows that jobs are no longer for life, many are surprised that they have to reinvent themselves. They may have to do so several times during the course of a career, and probably work later in life than they were expecting.

Career refreshment

This is a book that acknowledges the importance of finding the right kind of work. However, the job you love now may not be a job you want to do forever. Our motivations for work and our sense of the rewards we get out of it change as we grow older. Careers need to be refreshed from time to time. You may be required to change direction during your career, or you may choose to do so. Long-term, your focus may be on undertaking several roles you enjoy at the same time.

Working options

Organisations and workers are both learning to think differently about how projects are completed and work is delivered. We're all learning to think less about jobs and more about projects which solve an organisation's problems. Projects may be delivered entirely through external or internal staff resources, or a mix of the two. As this chapter will explain, the market is increasingly less focused on job-shaped objects. Don't overestimate the impact of this: most workers in the UK are still in conventional, 'permanent', employment. For every self-employed worker in the UK, there are almost six employees, and recent changes to tax regulations may mean that the number of self-employed workers may shrink, at least in the short term.

Many workers, particularly at a professional level, have learned to think and talk about their careers as a series of projects, rather than as long-term relationships. Hence the rise of terms like 'giganomics': when work feels more like a 'gig' or a one-off task, your focus is on multiple clients rather than a single employer. In addition, we have seen a growth in unpaid internships, interim positions, fixed-term roles, and zero-hour contracts.

Temporary and contract working

A significant slice of work is available on a **temporary** basis, largely through recruitment agencies. Although there are a few sectors which do not use temporary staff, most of the work available is in relatively conventional areas. So, for example, many office and reception roles are filled on a temp basis, as are a number of factory, warehouse, and processing Jobs. There are defined contract markets in health, education, and transport. In other areas it's more common for work to be provided on **contract**, sometimes for several months, particularly in fields such as IT. Temp work can be a good door opener by giving you knowledge of new sectors or what it's like to work in a large organisation. However, you may not get access to training and career development opportunities.

If you are going to take temporary or contract work, think about what it will add to your CV. You will subsequently be asked about your choices, and to make sure that you don't get stuck in temp roles for a long period, it's important to look at the learning value of each appointment. Remember also that undertaking work on a short-term basis is often an extended audition – because your performance is a known quantity, there's a pretty good chance that you will be offered a permanent role.

However, be aware that agencies match candidates and roles very rapidly, and it's easy to be pigeon-holed in the wrong way, for example, being offered a series of repetitive temp roles that don't stretch you. Agencies often assume you want to do what you have done before. Ask for different kinds of work assignments and negotiate learning opportunities.

Those recently qualified, and some career changers, find that paid or unpaid internships offer useful short-term opportunities. See Chapter 18 for more advice.

Interim roles

Interim work is essentially a form of short-term contract for more experienced staff. The work is provided through a wide range of interim agencies who regularly seek professionals with specialist expertise or extensive management or functional experience. The daily rate depends very much on the seniority of the last permanent job you held.

Interim professionals can cover a short-term problem or can be retained for several months or more (although with changes to UK tax regulations, very long-term interim assignments are disappearing). Unlike a consultant, your role is not just to make recommendations, but also to implement them. There is now a wide range of interim management consultancies in the UK, and if you are thinking of working in this field, investigate what they have to offer. However, the best course of action is to talk to someone who is currently undertaking interim work. Remember, too, that your most likely source of interim work is with an employer you already know.

An interim assignment is often a good way of gaining sector expertise that will allow you to move into a senior role in a new sector. These types of assignment offer a great deal of flexibility for those who want to work for part of the year and take extended breaks. The negatives are that you may have to work some distance away from home, and it's easy to become known as a 'career' interim and lose credibility as a permanent candidate.

Flexible working

Even in a recession, employers have become far more positive about flexible working, including some degree of home working, largely because of advances in technology. You may want flexible working hours because of family responsibilities, commuting stress, or to free up time for other activities. Part-time working can assist with life–work balance, but you will probably put in more hours than you are paid for. In addition, you may be under-exposed in the company and so not have a high profile with decision-makers, and therefore miss opportunities for promotion and career development offered to full-time colleagues.

Remember that a great many part-time jobs are negotiated rather than advertised, and these roles are often filled by word of mouth. Alternatively, a job that is first conceived as a full-time position may sometimes be renegotiated into a part-time role once you have proven your value.

Job shares can sometimes be the answer. However, it's nearly impossible to persuade an employer to agree to a job share unless you and your colleague are already working for the organisation. Employers are wary of set-up costs and the complexity of managing job sharers. Like part-time staff, job sharers sometimes find they are overlooked in career development terms. If your job-share partner leaves, you may find it difficult to find someone else to fill the role.

Mixed mode: employed and self-employed

Some workers mix salaried and self-employed work. A few have more than one employer. You may gain an income from freelance or session work. Investigate alternative careers by trying out something different. This might be at the weekend, or during the evening. We're used to thinking of work in terms of the '9 to 5', but some portfolio workers talk about the '5 to 9' week – work-related activities outside 'normal' hours of work. This is sometimes straightforward, and at other times less so when organisations expect staff to be available well beyond 5pm. There are, however, a range of mixed-mode options available. Some start businesses on a part-time basis, phasing one kind of work in and another out as the business grows.

Negotiating something that isn't a conventional full-time job

When candidates are talking to organisations, they often learn it's best not to talk about **job-shaped objects**. In other words, focus on the problem to be solved rather than the way the job is conceived.

When talking to an organisation, don't put your needs first. If you start by saying 'I'm looking for part-time/flexible hours', you draw attention to the time you won't be delivering. This can sometimes exclude you at the first stage of a selection process – it looks like you want a job that fits your lifestyle rather than the needs of the organisation. Focus on what really matters to the employer, matching needs point by point. If the employer is interested, you *may* have the opportunity to negotiate different working arrangements to those stated. Some employers would rather have someone on a flexible basis than miss out on the right skills; others are attracted by the ability to reduce overhead costs. If they want you, things become negotiable, including working conditions.

A portfolio career

What is a 'portfolio' career? The term is used to describe a deliberate choice to mix and match different work modes to find an effective balance. In the past, well-funded company pension schemes allowed executives to retire early and build a portfolio to keep them active during their final decade or so of working. Today's portfolio worker may have several drivers, including income, variety, and the difficulties and restrictions of salaried roles. Some hold down three or four appointments simultaneously, such as an IT consultant who also works as a board member of a health trust, a non-executive director of a publishing company, and a charity trustee. Some use high-paid working days to subsidise other work, for example, a marketing specialist who works for two days a week at corporate rates, the rest as a lecturer. Examples vary enormously: a self-employed joiner who buys and sells antiques as a side-line, a part-time HR specialist who works as a freelance book editor, an in-house lawyer who runs her own business as an equal opportunities trainer. Some of these people might not automatically recognise themselves as 'portfolio workers', but they are living examples of a new, pragmatic, and highly inventive method of working.

In recent years, portfolio working has attracted a great deal of attention. As indicated above, self-employment and part-time working remain important features in the UK and many other economies. Much of the increase in self-employment has been among those aged 50 and above. Home-based, self-employed contractors have done well in some industries, but in downturns can find that their work dries up quickly.

In the 1990s, only about 10% of executive career changers I was working with were interested in portfolio working. Today, it's more like 50% of men and women in this client group over the age of 50. Younger people, too, are adopting the approach – sometimes out of necessity – as Barrie Hopson and Katie Ledger make clear in their very practical book, *And What Do You Do?* (2009).

What kind of people benefit from this new working method? People who enjoy variety and change. People who have become dispirited by the constraints of a conventional career, lack of variety or growth. One of the great advantages of portfolio work is that you're not at the whim of a single organisation. You probably won't be made redundant, and if one income stream stops, you have others already in place. The exciting thing about portfolio work is its unpredictability: you never know what kind of project or enquiry is coming in next, and you may be doing an entirely different mix of work in 12 months' time.

Exploring new ways of working

1. Look seriously at how many things on your wish list you could achieve in a **conventional job** (for example, running your own profit centre within a larger organisation).
2. **Look before you leap.** Find people who have made a similar move. If it's a competitive sector, find people to talk to in other parts of the country.
3. Work out what **draws you** towards self-employment and what **pushes you away** (see Exercise 17.1 below).
4. Think hard about how you are going to **promote yourself**. How will people find you?
5. Plan ahead for **isolation** – recruit friends and mentors to support you, and network with people doing the same kind of work to swap stories and exchange ideas.
6. Focus on your **offering** – what product or service will you offer? How will it be different (cheaper, better, quicker, smarter) than others available?

7. **Don't get hung up on the frills**. It's great fun equipping your office, printing your own business cards, and setting up your own website, but none of this matters as much as your first piece of work. Look hard at where your first business transactions are going to come from.
8. Pin down your **first three clients**. If you have three customers lined up who will pay for your services, no questions asked, you probably have a business. Don't get hooked on the business idea: look for an income stream.

Beginning a portfolio career

The market doesn't offer you the chance of becoming a portfolio worker. It's not a role you can apply for. You might, however, begin a portfolio career as a result of a single request: if an organisation wants some of your time on a day-rate basis, you can start to think about how you are going to fill the rest of your week. This might not just be all about work – personal development and family time might be important ingredients too.

Dig deep in terms of possible elements in the mix. If you are already used to changing jobs rapidly and coping with varied income levels, the transition may be relatively painless. Think now, at the start of your exploration, about how you will fill your dance card so that you are busy and earning enough. If you plan it right, the work will find you, but that means you have to invest time and energy initially into making a great range of contacts (see Chapter 14 on networking as part of organised discovery). Learn how to talk about what you do: explaining your distinctive work mix, and actively seeking out people who can help you to find customers and other kinds of contact.

Check in with people who have made the journey before you. Talk to people who have successfully reinvented the work they do. The reality may not be as glamorous as you think. If you are head over heels in love with an idea, speak to at least one person who is thinking of getting out of that line of business. Find out why, then match that with a balancing conversation with someone who loves their new career. If you want to move back into permanent work later in your career, you will need to prepare a good interview answer about this segment of your work history.

Exercise 17.1 – Should I work for myself?

You might be considering self-employment, or perhaps finding a way to mix consultancy, contracting, volunteering, and other work in a portfolio career. How will you know if this career path is right for you?

The following questionnaire is designed to help you look at the pros and cons of such a move, looking at a mix of personal and practical considerations. Give each item a score between 0 'Disagree or Not Relevant' and 3 'Strongly Agree'.

Score how strongly you respond to each of the following statements.	Disagree or Not Relevant 0 point	Mildly agree 1 point	Agree 2 points	Strongly Agree 3 points
1. I'd worry that I'd only be as good as the last project I looked after				
2. I enjoy being considered an expert				
3. I need positive feedback and encouragement from colleagues and worry that I wouldn't receive that				

4. I feel it will improve my life–work balance				
5. I will always be worried about lack of long-term security				
6. I prefer to be master of my own fate rather than subject to the whims of an organisation				
7. I worry about having to constantly seek new business				
8. I will enjoy working for a variety of customers/client organisations rather than one employer				
9. I will miss the support structures of a large organisation				
10. I will value being in control of quality in every aspect of my business				
11. I don't want to deal with my own accounts and taxation				
12. I want to get away from bureaucracy and meetings				
13. I am concerned that working on my own might feel lonely				

14. I will enjoy working more on my own and being able to think and plan more effectively				
15. I need positive feedback and encouragement from colleagues and worry that I wouldn't receive that				
16. I feel it will give me an opportunity to increase my earnings				
17. I'm concerned about times when the money doesn't come in				
18. I will enjoy being able to translate hard work directly into earnings				

Add up your scores for all the **even number** questions (shaded text).	(T) Total **Towards** Score:
These answers give clues about the factors which **draw you towards** self-employment and possibly a portfolio career.	
Add up your scores for all the **odd number** questions.	(A) Total **Away From** Score:
These answers give clues about the factors which may **push you away from** self-employment and a portfolio career.	

Subtract your **(A) Away From** score from your **(T) Towards** score.	Difference **T – A** Score:

Interpreting your results

An overall score difference of +6 or above generally indicates a strong inclination towards working outside conventional employment. Even so, look carefully at the negative factors. What might get in the way of success? What can you work on?

Where you have a score close to zero, or even a negative score, and you are still interested in self-employment, you will probably want to review both positives and negatives in some detail. What does in fact draw you to self-employment? Are there factors not listed above?

Whatever your score, look carefully at those negative factors (odd number questions) where you have scored 2 or 3. What could you do to decrease the strength of these factors?

Now that you have a sense of the balance between the things that attract you to self-employment and the things that get in the way, look at the individual items in both parts of the questionnaire that you scored most highly.

What can you do to **increase** the strength of the things that **motivate** you towards self-employment or portfolio working? What can you do to **decrease** the strength of the things that **put you off** self-employment or portfolio working?

Looking for work after finishing study

'There is no such thing on earth as an uninteresting subject;
the only thing that can exist is an uninterested person'.

G.K. Chesterton

This chapter looks at ways of:

- Using this book if you're leaving full-time education soon
- Building on your academic achievement
- Seeking work when you have little or no work experience
- Translating what you know and can do into employer language.

Thinking through your options

When people finish one course, particularly at university, they often start another. Undertaking further study may seem the most comfortable option. Choose subjects for further study carefully. Avoid being press-ganged into a subject because someone else thinks it's a good idea or you're offered a place on a course. Will a new qualification enhance your CV and attract a higher salary? Is the course going to be personally fulfilling? And, if you are unsure about the answers to these two questions, are you just delaying the moment when you have to look for a job? Are you simply postponing a difficult decision?

What other options are there? Taking time out may appeal. Again, the question is whether you want to delay your career start merely to indulge yourself, to put off a decision, or are there things you really want to do? There is probably no other time in your life when you will have such freedom to travel, but think about what you will learn from the experience. Employers need to see the relevance of your time out, and what you learned from the experience. Sometimes you can successfully combine travel with work.

This might be the moment to begin job hunting. Perhaps this is the first full-time job you've ever applied for, or the next job after a career or study break. You now have a choice: do you make the same mistakes all new market entrants make, or do you shorten your job search time by working smarter?

Dipping your toes in the shark tank

If you've just finished studying, finding a job may seem a relatively undemanding task. After stretching your brain to think about quantum physics or linguistics, filling in online application forms and drafting a CV may seem brainless. This, of course, is why many of our smartest market entrants have weak CVs and unpractised interview skills: preparing to look for a job seems so easy, they don't do it at all.

There are several questions to think about if you've just finished a course of study:

- Are you looking for any kind of job to start repaying your student loan, or are you trying to build the kind of CV you'll be able to talk about with confidence in ten years' time?
- What kinds of roles might you be equipped to do, both immediately and in the future?
- Where are the jobs? How do you set about looking for them?

- What are the channels to finding jobs? Is it all about advertised positions, job boards, or networking?
- How do you apply the skills and knowledge you've learned in your studies? How do you talk about your qualifications in ways that employers find meaningful?

Getting more out of times you have seen work happening

Think about the information employers are most interested in seeing – evidence of working activity, and the skills you used. Look at times you have done any kind of work, or had even some small exposure to it: placements during an academic course, overseas work while travelling, paid work during term time, work experience while studying, holiday jobs, even workplace visits.

For any kind of work, paid or unpaid, dig into memory to remember what you learned, what you did, the contribution you made, and where you made a difference. Start to build up a detailed record, including job titles, company names, and details of specific projects. Aim to collect more evidence than you will actually need – so you can select the very best data for your CV, and so you have plenty of back-up material for probing interview questions.

While studying, collect evidence that you are employable, not just from work experience but anything you do that involves goals, challenges, team working, or organising. Take up opportunities for occasional or voluntary work – just a few hours can boost your CV. Work on your communication skills through group discussions so you become more confident when speaking. Skills such as the ability to manage social media need evidence to make them stand out, and remember that 'soft' skills such as negotiating or handling tricky customers are always useful even in an increasingly automated workplace.

Show how your experience is relevant to employers, and find topics to talk and write about with enthusiasm, as this shows commitment to learning and a 'can do' attitude. Try to choose a first job you find interesting, and one which offers you a clear opportunity to learn new skills and knowledge. Don't rely entirely on websites or career tests – talk to people who are doing the job.

When describing your strengths, avoid empty claims, but don't hide what you've done (see Chapter 7 on naming your skills and finding stories to communicate achievements). Draw out useful information when you describe your qualifications – what did you learn that is useful to an employer?

In your first CV, avoid clichéd adjectives or unlikely claims (see Appendix 2 for a model CV and a range of tips). Prepare for interviews rather than just crossing your fingers – see Chapter 16 on matching your abilities to specific roles. Make it clear you want *this* job, not just *a* job.

What to say if you have little or no work experience

When you are leaving full-time education, finding good-quality evidence for your CV can seem tricky. You may feel you don't have many skills, or you are not sure what an employer finds valuable. You may have a fairly good idea of your personal strengths and feel that these are the only things you can write about. You probably haven't yet really understood how to communicate your skills to an employer, and although you know that employers are interested in evidence of achievements, you don't feel you have many worth mentioning.

For all the reasons mentioned above, most school, college, and university leavers write an upside-down CV, where all the important messages are at the wrong end. You can read more about what goes wrong in my book *Knockout CV*, but the main point is that too many CVs major on recent academic success. These documents don't say anything about skills, know-how, and achievements until page 2, when a rather thin-looking work history is presented. Such a CV shouts out, 'I am a student who has had the occasional job', or 'I have little experience but some potential', rather than showing that you already have the skills to hit the deck running.

'I don't know what kind of work I want to do'

If you add up the thousands of hours students put into getting qualified, it's rather surprising how little attention they give to figuring out how they can apply their studies in work.

You may feel you are facing a bewildering range of choices regarding possible jobs and careers. Your problem may in fact be that you don't know enough about work to know which parts you are going to dislike. You may have little experience of work, or you may feel that your experience is not appropriate or useful to the new career you are hoping to begin.

Building career ideas if work is new to you

Stuck for an idea about the kind of work that will suit you? This is how you start:

- Begin by looking at two parts of life for clues: what you enjoy doing (how do you spend your free time and what activities motivate you?), and what you enjoy thinking/talking/learning about. Look at what you love doing and try to find the opportunity to try it out on a work experience basis.

- Look at all the subjects that have interested you, and translate them into potential sectors of work using Chapter 10.
- Review your work experience. What has motivated you or excited you? Where have you been fully absorbed in your work?
- Look at the subjects you have just studied. What would you like to know more about? What skills have you developed while studying? Be very clear about your qualifications: why did you study them, what are they, what did they cover, and what are your grades? But when you apply for a job, list them after your skills and work experience, however limited that is.
- Take work experience and short-term work assignments seriously. Write down the skills you used and what you learned.
- Conduct an audit: What do you actually know about work? How can you find out more? Who can you talk to? REVEAL interviews (Chapter 14) will help.

Finding out

Don't miss out on obvious sources of information. If you have studied at university, you will have access to a university careers service. In a society where funding is largely being cut from careers services, the university sector maintains high standards of support and guidance. You will get more out of your service if you go to all the careers events on offer and, when you have a one-to-one session, if you have specific questions about areas of investigation.

Lecturers and subject specialists can sometimes help with industry contacts, but one of the best sources of help for graduates, even if you left university some years ago, is the wide range of alumni associations available. Few current students seem to make use of alumni groups, and it's worrying how many graduates don't draw on their services either.

The great thing about an alumni group is that members have signed up to help others in the same network. Sometimes there are ground rules about how much to ask, and how often, but the real strength of these groups is that members have effectively pre-contracted to help you. You don't have to say much about who you are or why you are asking – simply mentioning that you're a member of the group is usually enough. An efficient association should be able to put you in touch with former students. Talk to people who graduated in your subject two or three years ago, and others who have found work in sectors you find interesting. Send an email to establish contact, but see if you can get a face-to-face meeting, or at least a phone call. Ask members of your alumni association to be your first point of contact for information interviews (see Chapter 14).

Accept all ideas for career pathways gratefully, but make up your own mind based on evidence. Talk to anyone you can reach out to who is doing work which looks interesting. Where your studies are related to work, use them as a platform for your investigation. Most organisations will speak to you, for example, if you are carrying out a research programme, as long as your questions are not too extensive.

Planning rather than drifting

Many people in their forties and fifties say: 'I wish I'd thought more carefully about career choice when I was young'. Your first full-time job makes a big impact on your career.

Many people take 'fill-in' jobs after qualifying. If you start that way, the danger is that you become a job hopper, snatching opportunities every time you feel dissatisfied, but never thinking about the overall shape and direction of your career. This experience can quickly lead to the idea that 'this is all there is' or 'this is what work is like'. You may convince yourself that the work you do will never be linked in any way to your studies. 'Fill-in' jobs can quickly become permanent posts unless you keep your goals in mind.

If you have little work experience, it's difficult to know what job satisfaction feels like. You don't get a sense of what motivates you until you've sampled work and experienced what 'fit' feels like. The advantage of traditional graduate programmes was that they allowed entrants to experience different parts of an organisation before choosing to specialise. The number of schemes has decreased significantly, but you can still adopt the career strategy of trying to replicate for yourself the opportunities provided by a good graduate scheme. Look for variety and range, particularly where you undertake unpaid work experience.

Make a smarter offer to employers

Employers are often asked what skills and qualities they consider vital for workers competing in the twenty-first-century labour market. Owning your transferable skills means applying *and* communicating them (see 'Translation', below). Often the focus is on self-awareness – being able to identify your own skills, values, interests, and strengths, seek feedback from others, and seek opportunities for personal growth. Other job profiles look for assertiveness and the ability to identify, create, investigate and seize opportunities, goal-setting, organising your time effectively, and project management skills. Finding opportunities is one thing – the next step is to match them with your core skills and knowledge. Graduate recruiters often look for the ability to sell or negotiate. In a rapidly changing world, employers are often looking for workers who are flexible and capable of adapting goals in the light of changing circumstances.

You could also think about the career survival skills you will need. Networking is important as a source of advice and information, as Chapter 14 demonstrates. Political awareness can also assist in the long term – being aware of hidden tensions and power struggles within organisations (sometimes defined as spotting the person most likely to stab you in the back).

Translation

The single biggest problem with CVs of university or college leavers is a failure to translate qualities, know-how, and experience into terms that are meaningful to an employer. This isn't just a problem for people leaving full-time education; people leaving teaching, the health service, or the armed forces face the same problem.

Get in the habit of 'bridge thinking'. Busy recruiters don't have time to make connections unless they're obvious. It's your job to form a bridge between your experience and the world of the hiring company. Get an employer to see not just skills, but *transferable* skills – and they only become transferable when you communicate them *in terms an employer will get excited about.*

For example, if you mention that you wrote a 6000-word dissertation, you will get little response. However, if you talk about why the topic fascinated you, the problems of gathering data, interviewing people, keeping up with the latest developments in your subject area, and working under pressure to achieve the project by a fixed deadline, then your interviewer starts to get interested. You have started to talk the same language.

Identifying achievements

Employers get tired of hearing empty claims about the abilities of candidates, but they get interested when you can provide hard evidence, especially if you've achieved something. This doesn't have to be earth-shattering like climbing Everest or winning an Olympic medal. Achievement evidence shows an employer that you like to get things done, and produce results which assist an organisation and add to your CV.

Your recent studies may provide useful material. Some academic subjects mean little to employers, so explain why the topics you studied are relevant to a modern workplace. Talk about what you most enjoyed in study, what it taught you in terms of life skills, what special projects you undertook. Even if you studied something fairly abstract, you will have gained considerable experience of researching, analysing, organising, interviewing, consulting, and presenting information concisely and coherently in speech and in writing.

Look at all of your experience for evidence of skills, learning quickly, and having the right attitude at work. Look at your activities outside study. Perhaps you organised complicated or exciting social events, competitions or sporting activities, or you may have been a member of a society or club. Think about the transferable skills that you acquired from these experiences, and make sure they are mentioned in your CV.

Taking unpaid work to build CV evidence

If you find it difficult to get a paid role, you'll almost certainly be offered opportunities to work for nothing to help you reach the first rung of the career ladder. At one time such opportunities were confined to highly competitive fields such as fashion or media, but now most large organisations have structured volunteer programmes. About 70,000 internships are offered every year in the UK, many unpaid. What impact does volunteering have on your career prospects? Does it make you look like a go-getter or a doormat?

Let's look at the downside. Even though you're working for an organisation with great values and purposes, you may still be stuck in a back room stuffing envelopes all day. In more influential roles the risk is that organisations place less value on your contribution and advice because they haven't paid for it. If you don't manage the event carefully or move on quickly enough, you can easily find yourself under-challenged.

You may give yourself CV problems if you stay too long or take too many internships. Research what your sector considers to be a reasonable length of time for an internship, and how many unpaid roles you can take without it looking like you are unable to secure a paid role. Keep in mind that while you are working, it may be harder to find time for an active job search. If there really are no paid jobs in your sector, you might be better off gaining experience in another, related sector for a couple of years.

One pitfall in working for nothing is that employers may leave you unsupervised while you undertake only low-level tasks. The critical question is what volunteering will add to your skills and whether it will enhance your value to future employers. Better placements include supervision, feedback, and development. Volunteer workers often recognise that they have a 'foot in the door': if a paid post comes up, you are a known quantity with a distinct advantage over external candidates.

All work is a deal, whether it's paid or unpaid. You may feel the deal is entirely one-sided as you're working for free, but it's still possible to seek a trade-off between your contribution and any non-financial benefits available. Spot them in advance and negotiate the ones that matter most to you. You could ask for feedback on your performance, a reference at the end of the assignment, and introductions to key people. Other spinoffs can include exposure to new contexts, learning and development, and useful CV evidence. In job interviews, don't say 'it was just voluntary work'. Good volunteering experiences can add significantly to your employability.

If you apply for a job and you're asked to work without pay for a period of time, don't be offended by the suggestion. Continue to show strong interest in the organisation. You might indicate that this mode of working isn't right for you at the moment, but you'd like to be considered for any paid roles that come up in the future.

Returning to work after a study break

Those who have taken a career break to take a full-time course need to plan carefully when trying to return to the workplace. Taking time out to study results in a gap in your CV, and doesn't always communicate employability; for a start, you have to convince an employer that you really are motivated to return to paid employment. You need focused answers to three questions:

1. Why did you decide to give up work to take this qualification?
2. What did you get out of it?
3. What do you hope to do next as a direct result of your studies?

If you fail to give an adequate answer to question 1, a recruiter starts to worry that you make random decisions in your career, or that you might be in danger of becoming a lifelong student. Question 2 requires you to think about *translation*, but also requires you to talk with enthusiasm about what you enjoyed while studying (after all, if you didn't enjoy it, why did you do it?). The third question requires you to communicate a clear, straightforward data burst about the way this recent experience adds to your CV and has helped to reshape your career path. (See also Chapter 15 on market readiness.)

'Must do' list: 10 steps to being job-ready if you're leaving full-time education

1. Your education may be the biggest recent event, but employers are only interested in your studies if they demonstrate useful skills or a high level of commitment. Explain your qualifications by showing how they taught you skills and knowledge useful in your next role.
2. Don't fill your CV with clichés and adjectives that scream out 'no experience, but great potential'.
3. Match claims you make about your skills with evidence. Give solid examples.
4. Catalogue any kind of experience that is work-related, including placements and volunteering. Look hard at the skills you used and where you made a difference. Use temporary work as a way of gaining skills and relevant experience.
5. Don't oversell your experience, but do explain it. Describe what you brought to the role, not just what the job description required you to do.
6. Plan for job interviews, don't wing it. List the requirements of a job and practise talking about your matching strengths.

7. Find someone with hiring experience to give your CV a cold read and to give you a general, introductory job interview. Prepare for it as if it's the real thing.

8. Reach out to people early in your job search. Ask around for ideas, leads, advice on your marketability. Talk to anyone who can move you closer to job-related information or a decision-maker.

9. Don't rely on job boards and advertised vacancies to help you find a job. You're far more likely to land your first role or useful work experience through word of mouth.

10. Take advice from people who regularly make shortlisting decisions, not random websites or the opinions of friends and family.

Master Sheet

The **Master Sheet** allows you to see the key ingredients in your ideal career on one sheet of paper. You can download this Master Sheet from the free resources section of www. johnleescareers.com – simply register to gain access.

Completing and using the Master Sheet

1. Transfer results from the exercises identified – see the relevant page numbers.
2. Make a copy before you write anything in the Target Sectors box.
3. On one copy, write down any ideas you can come up with for Target Sectors.
4. Show the other, incomplete, copy to trusted friends. Ask the question, 'what sectors should I be exploring?'. Write down their suggestions.
5. Review your Master Sheet frequently (try keeping a copy on the fridge door). Every time you look at it, you may see new ideas and connections.
6. Your goal is to come up with five target sectors to investigate, and then begin your enquiries. Pick up the phone and talk to someone who is easy to approach.

MASTER SHEET

My top 3 career hot buttons (p. 77)

1
2
3

3 important items from my Jigsaw Job (p. 39)

4 top skills (p. 84)

1
2
3
4

Relevant achievements (p. 92)

My 2 strongest work themes (p. 69)

1
2

My most important values (p. 114)

Subjects that fascinate me (House of Knowledge, p. 100)

Target sectors – 5 sectors I plan to investigate

1
2
3
4
5

CV and cover letter tips

Designing a winning CV

There are many ways of setting out a CV. The thing to remember is that your CV will only receive a few seconds of someone's attention before they decide whether to read further. This means that the first page of your CV does all of the work.

Decide if your CV ought to begin with a **profile**, a short paragraph outlining your background, top skills, and highlights from your work history. It says pretty much what you would say if you were in the room handing the document over. In general, if you're happy to stay in the sector you're already in, and just want the next job up, you may not need a profile and you can start with your most recent job. However, if you want to make a career change, you will probably need a profile to persuade the reader to consider your transferable skills before you get to your work history.

Look critically at the first two sentences in your CV. What immediate conclusions do you expect a reader will draw from those words? If you start by referring to background qualifications or experience which are not relevant to the role, you're immediately reducing your chances of being shortlisted.

This appendix includes an example CV in the style recommended by *Knockout CV*.

What to include on Page 1 of your CV

1. A CV only has one function: to get you a meeting. **Don't over-complicate it.**
2. Put your **contact details** at the top of page 1. Include an email address, and make sure it's appropriate ('pleasureaddict@slaphead.org.uk' or 'dad@smithfamily.net' do not convey a professional impression).
3. Write a **profile** if you want to make a career change. Mention your expertise, your main skills, the highlights of your work experience, and the sectors you've worked in.
4. Be careful how you **label** yourself in the profile. If you use a previous job title, that's what the market will offer you again.
5. Make your CV immediately **interesting**. The first 30 words matter.
6. Think of the first page of your CV as a **one-page advertisement**. A reader will make decisions about you before getting to the end of your first page. Make sure all *key information* is here.
7. Avoid **clichés** such as 'hard-working', 'team player', or 'highly motivated'. These just make you sound like everyone else.
8. Use summary words such as 'qualified' or 'graduate' to establish academic credibility.
9. List *relevant* **qualifications** and **training** on page 1.
10. Adjust the order of your bullet points so those matching the requirements of the job come top.

Other CV tips

1. Don't include anything that strikes a **negative** note, such as difficulties you had with a past employer, or a failed course.

2. Keep it **concise**. It isn't your life story.
3. Make the layout attractive, with plenty of white space. Don't print text so small it's painful to read.
4. Your CV should make **claims** about who you are and what you can do, and then provide evidence to back up those claims.
5. Express **achievements** in terms of awards, money, time, or percentages.
6. Vary the length of bullet points – make them easy to read.
7. **Translate** what you know and can do into terms that will appeal to a recruiter. Talk about solving problems, making a difference, etc.
8. Say something interesting about your **academic history**. Relate it to an employer's needs rather than regurgitating the syllabus; for example, if you led a seminar or gave a talk, write about your facilitation or presentation skills.
9. If you recently left full-time study, include information early on page 1 about your work skills.
10. Include 'interests' that show activity and enthusiasm, and those that have some relevance to the job.

Example CV

Jo Hope

Location: Newtown | m: 07777 000000 | e: jhope@example.com
LI: uk.linkedin.com/jhope27

A graduate information management professional with B2B experience focused on the information security needs of the insurance sector and a track record of achievement in building customer relationships:

- First-line technical support to business users.
- Redesigned user manuals and online customer support materials.
- Introduced customer satisfaction measurement.
- Launched a customer response programme during the COVID-19 epidemic.

EMPLOYMENT HISTORY

Information Security Manager –   Nov. 2019–Present
ZZ Technical Industry Group

Responsible for a team of five colleagues providing first-line customer response around data management and security.

- Improved customer satisfaction scores focused on my department's work by 38% in Q1 of 2020.
- Designed intranet staff training pages on internet security.
- Rewrote staff training manual.
- Seconded on in-house data security project for BigChain Plc.
- Designed and managed a customer response programme in relation to COVID-19 including weekly online FAQ updates.

Assistant Information Manager –   Jan. 2018–Nov. 2019
ZZ Technical Industry Group

Appointed to work alongside Information Security Manager in a
new department rolling out a range of new service products.

- Key input into product range launched March 2018.
- Commissioned web tools from outside providers.
- Recruited, trained, and coached new appointments, all retained
  as of 2019.

Customer Service Manager –   2016–2018
New Bubble Design

Taken on to provide and manage a range of customer service
functions including:

- Liaison with clients about design needs.
- Managing a team of freelance designers.
- Keeping projects on target and on budget.

Trainee Designer – AZ Holdings   2013–2015

Secured initial position against extensive competition as a trainee
in a prestigious major organisation offering B2B interior design
and shop-fitting solutions.

- Extensive client visits and consultations.
- My design for BetterShops front of sale literature featured in
  Print.
- Offered senior position but chose to move into consultancy
  work.

QUALIFICATIONS

Fine Art, BA Hons, Newtown University, 2.1, 2013

Diploma in Marketing, Newtown College, 2015

A Levels, Newtown Sixth Form College, History (A), English (B),
Art (A)

INTERESTS/VOLUNTARY COMMITMENTS

- Helped organise DesignFest fun run June 2017, raising money for children's charities.
- Active member of community group teaching digital photography/ Photoshop skills to retired groups.
- Wardrobe Manager, Green Room players, Newtown.

Features of the example CV

- The opening is brief and uncluttered. Do not title your document 'Curriculum Vitae', which sounds old-fashioned.
- It begins with a simple, user-friendly version of the candidate's name.
- In line with up-to-date formats, the CV does not include a full postal address but does include an email address and LinkedIn URL.
- There is just one phone number provided.
- It uses the word 'graduate' in the first line and saves more details about qualifications for later in the document.
- The profile avoids flowery language, too many adjectives, and unsubstantiated claims. It shows what this candidate might be doing next and headlines measurable achievements that will be set out later in the document.
- A short number of bullet points are used immediately after the profile to give early prominence to key areas of experience.
- Job titles are indicated in bold so that they stand out.
- It does not say 'I' or 'she' but adopts a punchy third-person style.
- Bullet points are used throughout; most begin with a strong verb.
- A short summary of the organisation and role is provided, leading quickly into more evidence of skills and achievements.

- It does not repeat obvious or dull information about past jobs, but emphasises hard evidence of added value. It pitches a strong message in the first half-page.

What you should *not* do with your CV

- **Don't** include information on page 1 unless it says something important that might get you an interview.
- **Don't** begin with information which confuses the reader about the kind of job you're looking for.
- **Don't** put yourself down, or try irony or humour. It rarely reads the way you want it to.
- **Don't** list referees. Provide details separately if requested. Talk to your referees every time you think they will be approached, and say why the role appeals to you.
- **Don't** use obscure abbreviations or jargon.
- **Don't** include your age or your date of birth.
- **Don't** disclose your salary. It's generally best to deal with this at interview or, if you have to, in a cover letter.
- **Don't** provide huge amounts of detail about jobs you did more than ten years ago.
- **Don't** send out poor photocopies. Print on good-quality paper if you are posting or delivering a copy.
- **Don't** include your reasons for leaving jobs, but be prepared to discuss this at interview in a positive way.

The essentials of a great cover letter

See *Knockout CV* for detailed advice on letter construction and for example letters.

- The only function of a cover letter is to get your CV read, and to get you a meeting. Make your letter **brief and focused**.

- **Research** – refer to the problems, opportunities, and headaches that your target company is facing. Work out the main requirements of the job, and provide matching evidence.
- Match the top five or six **strengths required by the role** using bullet points summarising your key experiences or skills. This short burst of information is the main content of your cover letter.
- Avoid beginning each sentence and paragraph with 'I'. Focus on the perspective of the reader.
- When you outline your evidence, word it differently from your CV; repetition bores the reader.
- Don't put anything in your letter that gives the reader an excuse to put it aside, for example, apologising for your lack of a particular requirement, or mentioning your age, or referring to negative aspects such as why you left your last job.
- Don't start 'Dear Sir' or 'Dear Madam'. Address it to a named decision-maker, even if your letter is **speculative** (to a company that isn't currently advertising a job).
- Follow employer instructions regarding the recruitment process carefully – mistakes at an early stage can easily get you excluded.

People who have transformed their careers

The case studies set out below are from clients who have worked with John Lees Associates and built their career change around ideas contained in this book.

Melissa Carr, Assistant Operations Manager, third sector

Melissa studied Archaeology and Classical Civilisation at Nottingham University. After leaving university she felt 'lost', not knowing what direction to take. She began a career within the ambulance service, which was not right for her but provided an early indication that she wanted a career where she could 'give something back and do some good'.

Melissa then moved from working in healthcare to childcare. After working in a school for children with learning disabilities, she felt she had found her niche. She writes: 'I loved going into school every day and working with the children. However, I did not want to go back to university to study teaching and I wanted more responsibility than being a teaching assistant. When I couldn't settle and decide what to do I decided to travel and work abroad, moving to Australia for two years. In hindsight this was perhaps an attempt to escape the real world of work and finding my career! I do not regret my time spent away and I had some excellent work experiences, but when I returned to the UK I felt more lost career wise than ever!'

Melissa's JLA coach asked for an outline of her dream job. Melissa writes: 'I just had to find it! I received guidance on creating a CV that would get me into an interview. My coach encouraged me to network rather than sit trawling through internet job sites. During this time I was temping as a waitress in a university, far removed from where I wanted to be! I felt demoralised when several job applications were rejected. I began to network in the university and through this I was given the details for the agency where I now work. I sent my CV, which I wrote using the advice in *Knockout CV*. Within a week I had an interview and within two weeks I was working as a support worker for children with autism. After two months I was promoted to management. I had found a job where I was giving something back but it also gave me the responsibility that I had craved.'

Melissa adds: 'I believe that having a clear idea of what I wanted from a job came across to my employers. They could see how passionate I was about working with children with learning disabilities. I have since moved on to other exciting roles in the third sector, building on the confidence I gained from my first big career change'.

Mary Wilson, musician and careers counsellor

Following a degree in Social Anthropology at Cambridge and an enduring curiosity in what makes people tick, work cultures, and how people behave in groups and individually, Mary was drawn to working in the advice/counselling sector and enjoyed developing her skills as a one-to-one adviser and group trainer in a number of different fields including the Citizens Advice Bureau, a national charity, higher education, and a psychology consultancy. Weaving through this time after hours and at weekends, she was also a musician performing in a band at clubs and festivals.

Taking a few years away from the job market, Mary brought up two children while continuing to perform in her band. The time came to think about a return to work and Mary spent a few months working through *How to Get a Job You Love*, having attended John Lees' career coach master-class. While Mary was comfortable with the idea of net-working and talking to people about what they do, she needed some time to focus internally on what really mattered to her and work out what she wanted to do next. 'I felt as if I was drowning in a sea of creative ideas and didn't know which direction to follow'.

'Working through all the exercises in the book gave me a space to think through my ideas and even encouraged me to have some more! The book does not force you to make decisions too early but allows for lots of blue-sky thinking before laying out all the exercises on a giant sheet of flipchart paper. It was during this final process that break-through occurred and I realised that I didn't have to decide between psychology and music but could see the links between them and gradually a vision emerged. I would be able to pursue a portfolio flexible career that also fitted around the needs of my growing family'.

After using the **JLA Skills Cards**, Mary commented: 'Although I have highly developed people skills, I am most inspired by taking a fusion of concepts/ideas/sounds into a forum where I am in command. I need to be out there being radiant, full of warmth and empathy with a box of delights at my finger-tips. The toolkit needs to be maintained from the inside (requires time alone) and is full of musical instru-ments, imagination, psychological concepts, and tools and ideas'.

Several years on from this process Mary enjoys a portfolio career, mixing family life, freelance career coaching, training, and regularly performing in her band – and she also devises and runs lively music groups for babies and toddlers. More recently she has expanded her toolbox to include violin teaching and sound engineering. Mary adds: 'Each year I look back at that giant sheet of flipchart paper summarising my values, interests, and skills and find they still have an enduring quality. While individual goals and outcomes might be differently tempered each year, understanding what really motivates, interests, and puts petrol in your engine is surprisingly similar today as it was seven years ago. HTGAJYL really kick-started this insight and I'm very grateful to have read it'.

Will Beale, Head of Network Operations Development, WWF

Will studied Natural Sciences and Chemical Engineering before joining Unilever. He worked in research, manufacturing, and new product development, but after ten years had a strong impulse to find his ideal career path. Will began by feeling apprehensive, but threw himself positively into the process: 'I spent three months undertaking information interviews with about 40 people in my target sectors. I learned a lot but uncertainty about the future meant it was also quite a tough time, especially for my family'.

Will applied for a wide range of jobs – business, NGOs, public sector. His dream was to work for an organisation focused on environmental sustainability and nature conservation. When a job at WWF (formerly the World Wide Fund for Nature) entered his sights, he felt he had found the perfect match: 'It seemed ideal but honestly I did not expect to get it. However, by this time my application, interview, and negotiation skills were well practised, and I knew how to sell the positive about myself'.

At WWF, Will has moved from quality management to building organisational excellence in conservation management. 'To the general public the WWF brand is strongly associated with wildlife protection', Will explains, 'but to achieve this we focus strongly on the underlying issues – such as climate change and drivers of unsustainable consumption. Whilst this makes the messaging more complicated, at every opportunity we try to recognise these connections'.

Will adds: 'What I love most about my work is when I have the chance to work with a particular project in more detail – for example, helping a team or organisation to develop a great strategy, or evaluating the impact of a major programme and considering how it needs to change. Over the last sixteen years at WWF, I have been fortunate enough to work with different offices and a wide variety of programmes in many wonderful places'.

James Voûte, Player Experience Manager, London

After studying English Language & Literature at university, James was drawn towards the publishing industry and built a 14-year career at a global academic publisher that culminated in a senior leadership position. Although he never took the role for granted, he wondered if he might have found a job for life. However, he left the company following an organisational restructure and, two months later, his father suddenly and unexpectedly passed away.

'My life was turned upside down', James explains. 'As well as the emotional upheaval of losing someone so close to me,

I went from what I thought was a stable and secure job to having no idea what I wanted to do next'.

James took some time out to plan the next stage of his career and approached John Lees Associates for career coaching as part of an outplacement service. By working through some of the exercises in *How to Get a Job You Love,* James was able to better understand what motivated him professionally and learned how to use his transferable skills to find a new role.

'My biggest problem was a lack of confidence', James remembers. 'Because I found myself with very little career direction and no recent experience in recruitment situations, I built up a lot of barriers and limiting beliefs in my head. John helped me challenge those assumptions and also to think about how to access the hidden jobs market'.

Through his personal and professional networks, James learned of a strategic marketing role in the games industry, at a company he'd always been keen to work for. 'As it turned out, the company had been looking to recruit for this position for quite some time and couldn't find the right person. Although I didn't have a background in the games business, I was able to demonstrate I had a lot of qualities that were transferable and present myself as a good match for the role'. He was offered the position and found he enjoyed the organisation's culture, building strong relationships with a new network of people, and growing his skill set in a different industry.

'Looking back at the situation, if you'd told me my next job after over a decade in book publishing would be a role called Player Experience Manager at a games company, I wouldn't have believed it', says James. 'It taught me that it's very easy to get defined by a strict set of beliefs and those beliefs can often be restrictive. By letting go of those preconceptions, I was able to grow both personally and professionally, and turn the corner during a very tough period of my life'.

Beth Grant, practice administrator, West Sussex

When she first came to JLA, Beth had been unable to work for three years following an accident at work resulting in a long-term shoulder problem. Initially, she could see very few work options and was worried about the kind of reception she would get from employers as a job seeker with long-term health problems and a long period out of the labour market.

Starting with JLA, Beth was encouraged by the fact that the exercises she was offered were tailored to her particular circumstances: 'All of the exercises completed were incredibly thought-provoking and were excellent in really helping you to think about what it is you want from a job and from life. Even though some of these were testing, with the amazing support I was fortunate enough to have, the end results far outweigh the difficult soul-searching moments'.

Not only that, the work she did boosted her confidence: 'At all stages we celebrated the progress I had made and it was refreshing to be reminded of how far I had come'. With her consultant's knowledge, advice, encouragement, and guidance, Beth found herself in a position to start looking at retraining and returning to work with a clearer understanding of her skills and the messages she needs to communicate to employers.

Beth learned to place the focus on what she can do rather than on her limitations, and in 2011 moved into the first permanent role since her accident, working as practice administrator in a busy, thriving orthodontic practice. Today, she describes herself as fortunate to have found an employer who values staff and customers equally, but also rewards hard work. She enjoyed the opportunity to return to work after the birth of her first child.

Beth adds: 'My self-confidence and self-belief have rocketed and using techniques I have learnt through my journey, I have confidence I will eventually find the right job for me at the right time. When I started career coaching I was struggling to even contemplate the thought of returning to some form of work and did not believe it would be possible to change this'.

More recently, Beth has started her own business making handmade sewn goods and running an online store. She adds: 'I feel thankful that my past experiences have allowed me to develop and have the confidence within myself (although there are frequent wobbles!) to take the bold step of selling goods I have made from scratch myself. I now have the freedom of working from home doing something I enjoy and having the flexibility to also be there for my family, along with the pride of knowing I've achieved something for myself, by myself!'

Simon Ryan, insurance research analyst and former TV location scout

Following a 12-month sabbatical after the birth of his son, Simon felt that he had reached an important crossroads in his working life. Having graduated with a construction degree, he'd worked in numerous sectors including construction, health and safety, event management, and property finance. Simon decided to investigate other options based on his skill set and experience. After a couple of unsuccessful meetings with recruitment consultants, he realised that assistance from a specialist in career redirection would be beneficial. Simon writes: 'I remember our first meeting and

John asking me a question: "when you're driving home from this meeting, what do you want to have happened to make you feel that it was worthwhile?"'

The answer presented itself as their discussions progressed, and they explored areas that interested Simon, and also importantly areas that hadn't in the past. They discovered that his interest in buildings and property could be transferred to the TV and film industry, particularly finding locations for filming. Simon decided that he would explore this idea further, and set about researching location management.

Simon continues: 'From the outside, the TV industry can be perceived as a closed shop that can't be entered unless you are in the know, but if you are determined enough, you can find a way in'. A chance conversation with a family member opened a door, and Simon started to make contact with various location managers.

The process was challenging: 'I gathered a list of people working in the area and contacted everybody in turn, with the initial purpose of asking them about their work, and any tips they could offer going forward, using the information interviews technique recommended. I was pretty much cold calling, which in itself was tough, but I persevered and it paid off'. Simon began to form relationships within the business, and after four months he got his first job as a location assistant on a production for the BBC. Since then he has moved back to an enjoyable role in financial services.

REFERENCES

Boorstin, Daniel J (1984) quoted in 'The 6 o'clock scholar: Librarian of Congress Daniel Boorstin and his love affair with books' by Carol Krucoff, *The Washington Post*, 29 January, p. K8.

British Psychological Society (2017) *Psychological Testing: A Test Taker's Guide*. Available online: https://ptc.bps.org.uk/information-and-resources/information-testing/guidelines-testing-and-test-use [accessed 12 February 2020].

Carroll, Lewis (1865) *Alice's Adventures in Wonderland*, in *Alice's Adventures in Wonderland and Through the Looking Glass*. London: Penguin Classics (2003), p. 13.

Chesterton, Gilbert Keith (1905) *Heretics*. London: John Lane, p. 16.

CIPD (2019) *UK Working Lives: The CIPD Job Quality Index*. Available online: www.cipd.co.uk/Images/uk-working-lives-summary-2019-v1_tcm18-58584.pdf [accessed 29 January 2020].

CIPD/Adecco (2019) *Labour Market Outlook – Autumn 2019*. Available online: www.cipd.co.uk/Images/labour-market-outlook-autumn-2019_tcm18-67336.pdf [accessed 27 January 2020].

de Jong, Tanja, Noortje Wiezer, Marjolein de Weerd, Karina Nielsen, Paulina Mattila-Holappa and Zosia Mockałło (2016) The impact of restructuring on employee well-being: a systematic review of longitudinal studies, *Work & Stress: An International Journal of Work, Health & Organisations*, Vol. 30, Issue 1, pp. 91–114.

Department for Education (2017) *Employer Perspectives Survey 2016*. Available online: www.gov.uk/government/publications/employer-perspectives-survey-2016 [accessed 27 January 2020].

Dickens, Charles (1860) *Great Expectations*. Ware: Wordsworth Editions (1992), p. 285.

Dickinson, Emily (1863) 'Poem 670', in *Poems of Emily Dickinson*. Boston, MA: Roberts Brothers, p. 203.

Emerson, Ralph Waldo (1840) *Essays: First Series*. Boston, MA: Phillips, Sampson & Company, p. 53.

Ferguson, Marilyn (1987) *The Aquarian Conspiracy: Personal and Social Transformation in the 1980s.* New York: J.P. Tarcher, p. 112.

Forster, Edward Morgan (1910) *Howards End.* London: Edward Arnold, p. 227.

Fox, Matthew (1994) *The Reinvention of Work.* San Francisco, CA: Harper Collins, p. 33.

Frost, Robert (1914a) 'The Death of the Hired Man', in *North of Boston.* New York: Henry Holt & Co., p. 14.

Frost, Robert (1914b) 'The Self-seeker', in *North of Boston.* New York: Henry Holt & Co, p. 61.

Herrick, Robert (1648) 'Seeke and Find', in *Hesperides, or the Works Both Humane and Divine of Robert Herrick Esq,* Vol. 2. Boston, MA: Little, Brown & Company (1856), p. 159.

Hopson, Barry and Katie Ledger (2009) *And What Do You Do? 10 Steps to Creating a Portfolio Career.* London: A & C Black.

Ibarra, Herminia (2003) *Working Identity: Unconventional Strategies for Reinventing Your Career.* Cambridge, MA: Harvard Business Review Press.

James, William (1890) *The Principles of Psychology.* New York: Henry Holt & Co., p. 333.

Jerome K. Jerome (1889) *Three Men in a Boat.* Ware: Wordsworth Classics (1993), p. 117.

Kipling, Rudyard (1896) 'If', in *Rewards and Fairies.* New York: Doubleday, Page & Company (1910), p. 175.

Lawrence, David Herbert (1928) 'Work', reprinted in *The Complete Poems of D.H. Lawrence.* London: Heinemann (1972), p. 450.

Layard, Richard (2005) *Happiness: Lessons from a New Science.* London: Penguin Books.

Lees, John (2013) *Knockout CV.* Maidenhead: McGraw-Hill Education.

Lees, John (2017) *Knockout Interview (4th edn).* London: McGraw-Hill Education.

Lees, John (2017) *The Success Code.* London: John Murray Learning.

Lees, John (2020) *Get Ahead in Your New Job.* London: McGraw-Hill Education.

Mental Health Foundation (2020) *Work–Life Balance.* Available online: https://www.mentalhealth.org.uk/a-to-z/w/work-life-balance [accessed 29 January 2020].

O'Connor, Sarah (2015) 'I quit! Job resignations and the UK labour puzzle', in *The Financial Times,* 25 March. Available online: https://www.ft.com/content/632649cf-fffe-3926-bde0-9e4497d7e01d [accessed 14 February 2020].

Office for National Statistics (2020) *Labour Market Overview.* Available online: www.ons.gov.uk [accessed 21 April 2020].

Pryor, Robert and Jim Bright (2011) *The Chaos Theory of Careers.* London: Routledge.

Reade, Charles (1870) *Put Yourself in His Place*. Boston, MA: Fields, Osgood & Co., p. 21.

Recruitment and Employment Confederation (2020) *Recruitment Industry Trends 2018/19*. Available online: www.rec.uk.com/research/recruitment-industry-trends2.

Resolution Foundation, The (2018) *The Kids Aren't Alright: A new approach to tackle the challenges faced by young people in the UK labour market*. Available online: www.resolutionfoundation.org/publications [accessed 29 January 2020].

Rohr, Richard (1999) *Everything Belongs*. New York: The Crossroad Publishing Co, p. 19.

Ruskin, John (1851) *Pre-Raphaelitism*. New York: John Wiley, p. 7.

Smith, Magdalen (2019) *The Grace-Filled Wilderness*. London: SPCK, p. 76.

Taylor, Matthew (2017) *Good Work: The Taylor Review of Modern Working Practices*. Available online: https://www.gov.uk/government/publications/good-work-the-taylor-review-of-modern-working-practices [accessed 29 January 2020].

Terkel, Studs (1974) *Working: People Talk About What They Do All Day and How They Feel About What They Do*. New York: The New Press, p. xi.

Twain, Mark (1905) 'A Humorist's Confession', *The New York Times*, 26 November.

Whitehead, Alfred North (1925) *Science and the Modern World*. New York: Macmillan, p. 4.

Wilde, Oscar (1940) 'Lady Windermere's Fan', Act 1 published in *The Importance of Being Earnest and Other Plays*. London: Penguin.

Williams, Rowan (1995) *A Ray of Darkness: Sermons and Reflections*. Lanham, MD: Cowley Publications, p. 152.

Wiseman, Richard (2010) *59 Seconds: Think a Little, Change a Lot*. London: Pan Macmillan.

Working Families (2019) *Modern Families Index*. Available online: https://www.workingfamilies.org.uk/publications/mfi2019_full/ [accessed 29 January 2020].

YouGov Reports (2017) 'Those aged 25–34 are unhappiest with work/life balance'. Available online: https://yougov.co.uk/topics/politics/articles-reports/2017/03/17/those-aged-25-34-are-unhappiest-worklife-balance [accessed 29 January 2020].

INDEX